Single Again—
This Time with Children

Single Again-
This Time with Children

A Christian Guide for the Single Parent

Alice Stolper Peppler

AUGSBURG Publishing House • Minneapolis

SINGLE AGAIN—THIS TIME WITH CHILDREN

Scripture quotations unless otherwise noted are from the Revised Standard Version of the Bible, copyright 1946, 1952, and 1971 by the Division of Christian Education of the National Council of Churches.

JB refers to The Jerusalem Bible, © Doubleday & Co., Inc., 1966.

MANUFACTURED IN THE UNITED STATES OF AMERICA

Dedicated in gratitude and joy

to my children

JEANNE, JON, JAN

who live Galatians 5:13:

"By love serve one another."

CONTENTS

PREFACE

This book took longer *not* to write than *to* write. It was easy to put it off. I was starting a single life again; I had extra pressures and responsibilities. And even after things settled down and friends encouraged me to put into print their experiences and mine with raising children alone, I procrastinated. Frankly, what little free time I had to myself I wanted to use in "living" life, not writing about it.·

Raising children, and especially as a single parent, is hard work. Sometimes the effort is all that registers. The joys and blessings are obliterated behind the personal weariness and frustrations. As the children grow older, we miss the beauty of that growth. Our daily prayers are reduced to "Help me—and them—make it through another day."

Perhaps the most unexpected blessing I've gained in writing these chapters is the awareness of the rich life God has provided me and my children, and the strong bond that unites us together and to him. We have something very special, and the accounts of our daily living have reflected its uniqueness. This awakening makes the prospect of each new day exciting. What depths of understanding, what additional joy, has God in store for each of us?

I thank my Augsburg editor for his guidance and patience in leading me to share some of my personal experiences on these pages, something I did not do in my original manuscript, and resisted *ever* doing. He led me to wait, and waited in turn, while God removed my self-imposed numbness to the pain you readers know as well as I. I'm also grateful to my mother, Hulda Stolper, for her loving encouragement, chapter by chapter, to continue in the self-revelation. As a single parent in widowhood, she has been the nurturing acceptor of me, as I, in turn desire to be to my children.

In writing books, as in raising children, it is God who deserves primary praise. This book is offered, therefore, in his name and to his glory.

In nomine Christe.

1

This Is Where
I Came In

It sits on my bedroom dresser—this large picture of me smiling. Sometimes it really gets on my nerves. At the end of a tiring day at the office followed by one or another problems with my three children in the evening, I scowl at it. "You have your nerve smiling. You should have *my* problems!"

SYMBOLS

But the picture remains. It's become a symbol of sorts. I had it taken shortly after my divorce when I didn't feel at all like smiling, but the photographer insisted. When I first got it, I used to say to myself, "Someday you'll smile like that again, Alice. Someday. When everything is all right again."

I'm not sure everything will be all right again, not in the sense I meant at the time. Life is a series of trade-offs. Married—not married; parent—childless; whatever. There is no life we can live that puts everything in the "Wonderful" column and nothing in the "Not-So-Wonderful."

GAMES

Have you ever "played God"? Have you ever known all the answers: what's best for you, what's best for your loved ones? Ever fool yourself that because you have faith and trust in God that your prayers are objective and you've placed your life completely in his hands, when really *you're* basically deciding all the moves?

I have. I'm very good at "playing God." I don't realize it when I'm doing it of course, or I rationalize myself out of suspecting it, but I've played it again and again in life. The trouble with "playing God" is that one never wins. Or at least one never wins true joy. I have a sign on a closet door that reads:

Happiness is like a butterfly.
The more you chase it, the more it will elude you.
But if you turn your attention to other things,
It comes and softly sits on your shoulder.

I never realized that as a child, and I keep forgetting it as an adult.

I think I've known all the answers in my "playing God" game since as long as I can remember. When I was in first grade, I knew I'd be a teacher. And of course I'd get married and have children. As a matter of fact, the best time seemed right after college. Find a husband and have children at a young enough age to be able to grow up with them. Why wait? It seemed so simple back then.

And so I got married. And I taught first and second graders in a Christian school. In thinking about writing this book, I recalled the first time I taught the children the story of Noah's ark. Naturally they had a lot of questions. One question stumped me, however. Why was it that after the ark was loaded, *God* closed the door behind Noah? "Didn't the door have an inside doorknob?" one child asked. "Couldn't God trust Noah to close it?"

Soon the entire class was discussing the "problem." I was amazed at the analogies the children made to their own lives.

"Maybe Noah was afraid of the dark and would have kept the door open a little bit to let some light in," volunteered one student. "Maybe God was afraid Noah would forget because as soon as he got in the ark he'd play with the animals," said another. Finally one pensive boy stopped all queries with his irrefutable reasoning. "I bet God closed the door from the outside to make sure it stayed closed!" he said. "When *my* dad closes my door, that's what *he* means."

"And Yahweh closed the door behind Noah" states Genesis 7:16 (*JB*). God shut the door—tight! That was the end of it. The life Noah had known to that point was over. When the door opened again, a whole new life would begin.

That's the trouble with "playing God." Just when you've set up the gameboard the way you want it, God—the real God—may decide to slam a door in your face. It makes life—life the way we've planned it—very frustrating! Oh, God may have his reasons for the illness, the death, the divorce, the loss of job—but who knows what they are at the time, if ever? "Unfair!" we shout, thinking of games in which the rules never change without warning.

The Creator doesn't play by our rules. He rules by a love and knowledge we can't attain. When he closes a door, or allows it to be closed, he has a reason. And even when the immediate end seems disastrous, he promises good can come from the evil. For "we know that in everything God works for good with those who love him" (Rom. 8:28).

DOORS CLOSING

I was the mother of a newborn child and a three-year-old upon my first real experience with doors closing. My husband left; my marriage ended. Just like that! Or so it seemed at the time. Almost overnight everything I had known, was comfortable with, believed in, was over. *Over!* I couldn't believe it. I didn't accept it. I kept seeing rays of hope, beams of light through the closed door. I couldn't believe the God of my childhood, my youth, and early married life would let this happen to me. Or if to me, certainly not to my young children.

I sat rocking the baby as my husband took his last load of personal belongings out into the early dawn of that humid July 18th, years ago. I turned the swivel rocker away from the door so as to avoid seeing his departure. But I couldn't escape the sound of the lock catch as the door closed quietly. I was weeping. My infant son, nestled in my arms, slept peacefully—unaware. I held him tightly, both giving and taking comfort. The drab, empty wall I faced seemed symbolic of my future. I was in a state of shock. I didn't know where to turn, what to do next.

The following two years passed like twenty. For every step I took forward, it seemed I slipped three back. I experienced continual emotional and physical anguish. I learned to know, like the psalmist, the pits of depression and despair.

Month after month passed, yet nothing seemed to change for the better. I continued Sunday worship, but quit reading the Scriptures. Little in them comforted me anymore. I believed in God, yet often disagreed with him. He had opened a door to a wonderful new profession, a job I really enjoyed. Yet he hadn't reopened the door of my marriage. And in addition, I wasn't moving along fast enough on my personal gameboard of life. It was taking too long to heal. God may have had eternity in which to solve problems, but I didn't. My children needed a "whole" family. I needed a husband. Wasn't this God's plan? Wasn't this the biblical ideal? My children were at the most impressionable age. Why was God delaying in making life better for them?

"You're strong! You'll survive!" my friends and family kept saying. How I hated that. I didn't feel strong. I was at the fray of my emotional rope. I was drowning, gasping for air. I was on a tightrope with no net in sight. Yet people kept saying confidently, "You'll make it." What did they know, really know, about what I was going through? Their lives seemed sheltered, unreal. Their words echoed superficially across dark chasms. They were willing participants in a facade of rose-colored illusions. Their very attitude seemed a mockery of reality.

In the long run they were right. Their prayers were always with me, and they knew God would see me through this trial somehow. But at the time, I couldn't comprehend, let alone accept, this fact. God was a being who floated in and out of my life, sometimes vividly colorful, imparting great strength; sometimes merely outlining a faint shadow, thoroughly draining me. Yet even when I could barely make him out, Christ was always there. He pursued me relentlessly. He followed me everywhere, the Hound of Heaven.

After two years, I remarried. My husband adopted and raised my children as his own, and God blessed us with another. For the first six years of this marriage, life seemed normal. God had seen it my way at last, and after all, wasn't my way based on his revelation? My children were healthy and happy, and I could even continue my editing profession, partly at the office, partly at home. Yes, I was doing well at the marriage and family game—so well I could engage in "playing God" once in a while, perhaps more than not.

One day we were the average, "normal" family of five; the next day we were not. For the sake of all involved, I offer no explanation of that statement. But once more I was sent reeling. And it was just the first of similar experiences. Had I not known fear—total panic—before, the most drastic of them might have overwhelmed me, but God has always sustained me in real crises. He flows in and takes over completely until mind and body are over the shock and once more able to function.

For the next four years God was my only confidant. When my first marriage failed, I could turn to my pastor. This time, for many reasons, I chose to keep the door to the clergy tightly closed. But God was enough. He talked—in so many ways—and I listened, really listened. I tried to follow his rules as I stumbled along the gameboard, looking with hope to the professional aids I found along the way. But finally I realized the only real help was another closed door, another new life.

If you think living with and explaining one marriage failure is difficult, try two. Only God knew the reasons; I gave none to family or friends. If they thought less of me, it didn't matter. God remained my source of strength.

DOORS OPENING

After my first divorce, I had begun a new profession because of financial necessity. In addition, I wrote poetry, which served as personal therapy, and took some dance lessons as a challenge and a diversion. I did a great deal of self-study and faced up to traits I had never liked in myself. With daily prayer and resolve I slowly changed in many ways. As promised, God had brought good out of evil. I began to see a reason for God's slamming that first door in my face. Perhaps it wasn't God's reason at all, but it was enough for me. I liked the changes it had forced me to make. I liked myself better now; I accepted myself. And in beginning to love me, I could better follow God's command to love others as myself. I also learned from the experience that love was the most important gift I could give my children.

In addition, my new work broadened my life. It enabled me to pursue new interests and to use latent talents. In every way my life had been unexpectedly enriched—all because a door had slammed. It was a "forced" enrichment for which I've never ceased to be grateful.

Thus when another marriage ended, I knew blessings could follow the grief. It was at this time I decided to have my photograph taken, along with family photographs. The children were not enthusiastic over the latter, but I knew someday the pictures would mean much to them, and my prediction has already come true.

I would "smile" again. One way or another, I was convinced of it. During the last year of this marriage God had opened the door of a related professional field, and I went through eagerly into a marketing position. Many of my new associates were former athletes who saw life much like a game of football. No matter how hard one was hurt in a play, one always tried to go right back into the next play. The only alternative to playing was to sit out the game on the bench. Their outlook made sense. There was no time to be wasted in self-pity. One had to grit one's teeth and go right back into the game of life, or otherwise it would pass one by.

Four years have gone by since that divorce. I smile often, and sometimes I cry. I cry far less, however, than I smile. I really do like that photograph of me smiling. It usually gives me a lift and makes me smile in return.

I once read that God never closes a door without opening another. In my life he has opened many, many more than he's closed. And his personal door is a double door, like those in adjoining rooms in hotels. I have closed, even locked, my side of the door to him more than once. Yet whenever I've opened it in panic, needing his immediate presence, or just unlocked it, peeking in to see if he's still there, the other door—his door—is always wide open. It is a frightening, awesome thing. It is an overwhelming evidence of unconditional love. It reminds me of the Shakespearean sonnet framed above my desk, "Love is not love which alters when it alteration finds." Only our Lord's love "never alters."

During these past few years I have learned to know and love my children far more than I ever thought possible. We are very close, although we differ from one another and disagree freely. For my part, I understand them better now because they are older and can express their feelings and rationale in adult terms. On their part, they probably are so understanding and supportive because they themselves have gone through more than most of their peers. Their lives have had multiple upheavals; they've been unduly complicated and emotionally upsetting. When the doors slammed on them, the children were younger and had far less resources of life to fall back on. But from the beginning they had Christ, and in different ways he touched each of their lives in their own language.

I'm not sure what credentials one needs in order to write a book about raising children alone. I am not a clinical child psychologist; I am a mother, with no special training. But if experience counts, I surely have some. I have raised children singly at preschool age, and from fifth grade into college. I've been extremely blessed, however, in that the loving support of the children's father, who helped raise them during their formative years, had remained a vital and active factor in their lives. I realize this situation is rare; it is a door God has kept open.

Many of my friends are now going through a divorce after twenty-odd years of marriage. We sit and talk. We comfort and help work out each other's problems. I've known them for years. I don't know you at all. All I know is that we have something in common. This book is filled with advice—hints and suggestions in raising children singly that my friends, I, or acquaintances have found workable. But none of us always know what's best for *our* children, let alone yours. It's impossible to write a book for all situations. I can only share, and then pray that you find yourself *somewhere* on these pages.

Life keeps changing—for you, for me, for everyone. We can count on that. There is no way to stop change in our lives. But God's love never changes. We can be assured of that. And for every door God closes, he *will* open another.

"Behold, I have set before you an open door, which no one is able to shut" (Rev. 3:8).

2

Single,
But Not Alone

Being single. It's not so unusual. You spent your childhood and youth as a single person. Sometime during your adult life, you married. But if you had stayed married, and are female, the odds are you would have outlived your husband. You would have both entered and left this life as a *single* person.

SINGLE IN SOCIETY

Statistics show that 40% of the U.S. adult population is single. That's a higher percentage than most of us realize. Four out of every ten Americans 18 and over are *single*. For every *three* couples, there are *four* singles!

Of this adult single population, about 25% are ages 18-30, 61% are 30-65, and 14% are over 65. And 60% of all single adults are women. Thus you are hardly alone in your "single" state.

And believe it or not, neither are your children. The number of children living in single-parent families tripled in the last 20 years, and continues to rise. In 1980 there were an average of

6000 marriages performed every day in the U.S. Daily, also, were 2000 divorces. Trends indicated this 33% divorce rate will increase to 50% in the next few years. In the 1970s approximately 20% of all children were living in one-parent homes. Yet as more marriages end in divorce, it is estimated that 45-48% of all babies born in 1980 will live with only one of their parents before they are 18. *That's almost half!*

SINGLE IN THE CHURCH

"If there are so many of us single Christian parents around, then why do I feel so alone?" asked Connie, a newly divorced friend of mine. "I don't even like to go to church anymore. I don't feel part of the group. I sit there alone with my children, and it seems like there's a big sign in bold letters over our pew that says, NO HUSBAND! NO FATHER! Sometimes I can't wait till the service is over so I can escape from the stigma."

"I don't feel that way," piped in Barbara, "but I do turn off during the sermons. Maybe I'm paranoid, but every week it seems the sermon is marriage-oriented. My minister's wife just had another baby, and if I hear one more sermon on how wonderful marriage and families are, I'll scream! How can my pastor be so insensitive? I mean, I sit right down in front, in his full view. If he were an older man, I might understand it, but he's not. He's young! And I'm not the only single divorced parent in his congregation. I don't feel he's purposely forgetting me, neglecting me, but I feel he's *blind* to me!"

I understand their reactions. I've lived through them. Like other Christian single parents, I have vivid memories of attending church with spouse and children. Sometimes it's still painful to attend without a mate. Whether the congregational members show genuine friendliness, are apathetic, or are even gossiping behind one's back, it hardly matters at times. All conditions can bring an ache, especially when one first returns to single life.

My most "difficult" time during church services is when prayers are raised in thanks for marriage anniversaries. Do you realize how many married couples are in an average congregation? If each one wants a prayer offered each year, barely a Sunday goes by when worshipers are not asked to thank God for the couple's good fortune. It is at times like this when one's Christian love is brought to test. One is tempted to cry, "How about a prayer for me? How about the years I've raised my children alone, without the benefit of a loving mate's assistance? How about thanking God for helping me through these years of Christian family living— *alone?*"

But back to Connie's question, "If there are so many of us single Christian parents around, then why do I feel so alone?" Well, first of all, although it's true there is a 40% single population in our country, it's not correct to assume there are "so many of us single Christians." As a matter of fact, about 85% of adult singles are *not* religious, or at least not practicing their religion. If you are curious about your congregation, take a count of the singles on the official membership list. Then take a count on Sunday morning. You'll find many Christian singles may be on the books, but they are not in the pews.

Why this irony? Why, just when a person needs a "family" more than ever, is he or she inclined to withdraw, at least psychologically, from the church family?

Some of the reasons were given in my friends' reactions to church services now that they are divorced. The fact is that divorce is not recognized in the church. Death, illness, and all the "honorable" misfortunes of life are raised at the altar of God, and the congregation is asked to bow their heads and pray along with the minister for this or that Christian in pain. But rarely is a congregational voice raised to heaven for the pain of divorce. No church prayer is lifted for an individual who is going through what medicine considers the second greatest stress for any human being. The church, which prides itself in its caring, is blind to a larger and larger group of Christians each year. *Divorced people are its forgotten people.*

Sometimes it seems difficult to remain faithful to the Lord when you feel his people don't accept or understand you. But if you search the reasons for the "neglect," it's usually not because of nonacceptance. Divorce is so common today that almost every Christian has a divorced person for a relative, friend, or neighbor. No, most Christians accept the Christian single parent; they just don't understand him or her. They are uncomfortable with someone being single during the "marriageable years." They truly don't know how to react.

Along with lack of understanding comes acceptance of stereotypes. Society still generally considers a single parent home a "broken" home. I can understand that stigma from society, but I experienced pain year after year filling out a Christian school application form for my youngest and always finding the same question on the second page: "Is this child a product of a broken home?" "A *broken* home?" I used to question. "What do you suppose constitutes a broken home in our Lord's eyes? The loss of a parent? Is it not rather the loss of Christ's presence? Can *any* home be broken if the Lord is its head?"

One of my friends is always quoting Eleanor Roosevelt. We kid her that we don't remember Eleanor, but she goes on undaunted. Barbara thinks the church is patronizing. In hearing my "broken home" story, she said that's what her marriage was *before* it dissolved. She suspects it may even be true of the "complete" family that sits in the pew in front of her every Sunday. But her point is, a broken home is not yours, not anyone's, unless you let it be. Eleanor Roosevelt once said that no one can make you feel inferior without your consent. Thus if your Lord does not label you, do not allow anyone—*anyone*—else to.

If Barbara is correct, and the church is patronizing, it is also waking up and changing. Singles—you and I—must continue to speak up to help the church understand and recognize us. Organized Christianity is slowly facing the fact that for many the single life is not just a temporary passage from childhood to the "more acceptable" state of marriage. *Being single for millions of adults is a permanent way of life.* The American Lutheran Church made singles their "special concern" in 1978, and in the same year the Southern Baptists started a two-year campaign to reach single adults. Similar activity has begun in Presbyterian and Roman Catholic churches.

SINGLE WITH GOD

But once more let's return to Connie's question, "If there are so many of us single Christian parents around, then why do I feel so alone?"

Alone. Have you ever felt this alone? According to research, death is the most traumatic experience in one's lifetime, for it is completely irreversible. But divorce is also shattering; it is essentially the death of a relationship. Most of us know we're supposed to mourn for the dead, but little is ever said about mourning the living. *Yet divorce brings a feeling of bereavement just as overwhelming as death.* To recover, one has to go through a period of mourning during which one first must acknowledge the grief, and then struggle to go beyond it.

Katie, another friend, understands the total depression of feeling all alone. When her marriage was breaking up, she struggled to put her life completely in God's hands, but for a long time was gripped with fear—the fear of facing the future alone. No words could comfort her. After a while the loneliness and fear turned to anger: anger towards God for allowing her divorce, anger towards her husband for leaving her, anger towards herself for not being able to keep the marriage going. And when Katie attended church, she felt an additional negative: a sense of guilt. She felt that because she was lonely, depressed, fearful, and angry, she must not have enough faith, enough commitment. At first this

25

produced spiritual panic. Later it turned into disinterest in Christianity. She just didn't care. And yet not caring made her feel even more guilty.

Many psychologists believe that fear is one of the greatest blocks to self-esteem and self-fulfillment in people. Afraid of failure, most humans tend to follow the "safe" path, to conform to what others think and do. This was Katie's situation. She had never experienced a happy, fulfilled life as a single person before marriage. She had never let her unique personality evolve apart from that of her parents and her mate. She had conformed at an enormous cost—losing sight of her real needs, her real self.

It was a study of Psalm 139 which gradually brought Katie back to spiritual life.

> O Lord, thou hast searched me and known me!
> Thou knowest when I sit down and when I rise up;
> thou discernest my thoughts from afar.

All the verses of this psalm started to sink in. God knew *her,* knew her before she had been conceived. He knew everything she thought before she thought it; he knew all her actions before she acted. Again and again she read that psalm until finally she learned that God accepted her the way she was. And when she accepted that fact, she could accept herself. She could be Katie and still be a child of God. The fear of going on alone began to leave. "Be strong and of good courage; be not frightened, neither be dismayed; for the Lord your God is with you wherever you go" (Josh. 1:9).

Barbara experienced loneliness after her divorce, but little fear. Barbara is one of those people we all wish we could be. Quoting Eleanor Roosevelt again, she said, "Look fear in the face. You must do the thing you think you cannot do."

Nevertheless, Barbara had to come to grips with living her life alone. What helped her was the realization that we're all alone at various times of life, no matter *who* is with us. "I essentially gave birth alone," she said. "No one else went through my labor pains for me. Later this son I birthed had to go off to Vietnam alone. And there he died in action, virtually alone. *Alone.* And now my ex-husband has to face cancer alone. Oh, he's remarried. But the cancer is his, and only he will feel its physical pain."

Barbara does not really believe a Christian is ever truly alone, however. Her favorite psalm is Psalm 23: "The Lord is my shepherd." She lets God do her fearing for her. She lets God lead her through the frightening shadowy valleys to the green grass of restored strength. She renounces the world's fear and embraces Christ's peace instead. "Peace I leave with you: my peace I give to you; not as the world gives do I give to you" (John 14:27).

SINGLES' CALL FROM GOD

Connie, Barbara, Katie, and I have discussed God's call to single parents and know that we are not to neglect the "one thing needful" (Luke 10:42): we are to raise our children in "the discipline and instruction of the Lord" (Eph. 6:4). We are the worship leaders in our families and are to share the gospel, indeed to live by it, by both word and example.

"I came that they may have life, and have it abundantly," says our Lord (John 10:10). *He requires no conditions for his abundant life.* He does not say it's ours *if* we're married, *if* the church recognizes us, *if* society accepts us. There are no *ifs.* Nothing. He simply says that *we*—with all our sins, all our sorrows, fears, shortcoming, losses—*we* might have it abundantly.

So now there is a reason to participate in the life of the church —yes, even when it is not meeting all our expectations. Now it is easier to decide which activities to join and which not. The choice is for those that help us grow in our own spiritual lives, and in which we can participate with our children.

I have friends who ask, "How do you get your children to attend church with you? Mine stopped in high school. They just sleep in."

Well, some things are just assumed in family life. How did you get your children to go to school? Wasn't it just assumed? Was there ever any question about it? My children knew from little on that they'd all learn to play piano just as they'd all learn to read. After taking piano, they could tackle another musical instrument. It was never a negative suggestion; it was a positive one, something to which they could aspire.

Attending church was a similar natural outcome of early training. As babies, I carried my children around the apartment, stopping at pictures of Jesus. I identified our Lord; I talked of his love. I didn't know if my infants comprehended, but I gave the information nonetheless. I rocked the children, singing children's Christian songs to lull them to sleep. And though their actions often disturbed my worship, I took them to church from the beginning.

Church attendance became a pattern—a way of life. Had I adopted older children or raised those from a husband's first marriage, I would have begun the pattern at whatever age the children were. It's never too late to begin Christian training. The Holy Spirit's power will work faith at any age.

During his sophomore year in high school, my son commented that some of his friends no longer worshiped. He said he still wanted to, but what if he *didn't* want to? Isn't the gospel a gift? Should worship be forced upon someone? Isn't the "forcing" making it law rather than gospel? As an adult (as teenagers see themselves), shouldn't he make the decision, not I?

Good question. He had a point. I could only answer the truth, that I took my call of parenthood as one from God. I sincerely believe I will be called on someday to give an account of my raising the children in the love of the Lord. And as long as I have the responsibility—as long as the children live under my roof and are supported by me—he and his sisters would have to live by my rules, by my conscience. When they were on their own, they could take this great responsibility for their souls' nurture on themselves. But for now, they would be causing me to go against my conscience if they did not follow my example.

I simply told the truth. And it was accepted and respected, just as my children's feelings are expressed truthfully, accepted, and respected. And so we attend church together.

In addition to formal church worship, one can't underestimate the value of daily prayer within our single-parent families. Katie listens to her younger children's morning and evening prayers. Barbara's family joins in singing their prayers. I've learned to pray aloud for all my children, not only in the silence of my room, but in their presence, after a meal for example. There is nothing more beautiful to hear than someone you love thanking God for you and praying for his blessings in your life.

If you have never prayed anything but formal prayers in your home, consider substituting one of your own. "Thank you, God, for giving me my children. They are the best gift I have," is an example. Just 15 words, but if your children have never heard anything like them, they could be the most meaningful words they've experienced.

Children of a single parent are often very perceptive and protective of that parent. Mine are. After experiencing two marriage breakups, they feel they have only me to really count on, and they are very watchful that all is well with me, because anything that affects me is likely to affect them also. Sometimes I think they feel guilty—needlessly, but true nonetheless—that they are a burden to me or a cause of anxiety. So to know that I turn to God for strength gives them strength. Even if children (especially teenagers) "reject" God, it gives them security to know we single parents don't. You and I are much more of a model than we can imagine. Though rebelling periodically against our values, our children respect them because of our constancy.

Family devotions is another worship opportunity from which

much good comes, going beyond the spiritual to the strengthening of interpersonal relationships. If children and parent take turns in leading a family devotion, they'll learn a great deal about one another in addition to strengthening their faith.

As with prayer, it's important to keep the devotions simple and to allow the children to react as individuals. One of mine likes to write a "creative" devotion; another prefers to read a formal message from a devotional booklet; the third usually wants to talk about an incident from school or social life and apply it to our spiritual life. Sometimes scrapping the devotion to talk about something on a child's mind leads to a more meaningful worship experience.

"Being single. It's not so unusual." That's how this chapter begins. As a single parent, you are not a rare species in society, *or* in the church. And your life will not always remain in limbo.

What is a single-parent family? It is what a single parent decides to make of it. It is what the family asks God to make of it.

"Whatever you ask in prayer, believe that you receive it, and you will" (Mark 11:24).

3

Children—
The Unwilling Victims

The little girl stands in front of a greeting-card rack with her mother. She is looking for a special card. She sees every type imaginable, but not the kind she needs. The child goes home and prepares her own card. She takes out her crayons and draws a picture of her mommy and daddy together on a large sheet of paper. Then she takes her scissors and cuts the card in two—right between her parents.

The child needs a card for divorce. She has just experienced it. She wants to send each parent a special card. And so with great love she writes *her* simple message of love on each of the two cards she's made.

Such is the theme of *Two Special Cards,* a children's book by Sonia Liker and Leigh Dean. Such is the reality of more and more children's lives each day.

CHILDREN'S REACTIONS TO DIVORCE

Little Hazel, the girl in the book, did not want the divorce. But it happened anyway. Most children do not want their parents to

31

divorce. But it happens anyway. And most children are given no warning. They may consciously or subconsciously note conflicts within their parents' marriages, but generally the separation and divorce itself comes as a shock. What do children *feel* when their lives are so drastically changed? What are their *fears?* How do they *react?*

Many of our children's feelings, fears, and reactions are the same as ours. But in some way they are distinctly dissimilar, or they manifest themselves in different ways. We sometimes become so involved in the problems we experience, so wrapped up in getting ourselves together, that we don't take time to truly analyze the problems our children face. Or perhaps we don't feel qualified to do so.

This chapter recounts typical children's responses to the permanent absence of a parent in their homes. It is a beginning point in a book about single-parent family life. We need to understand where our children are emotionally at the present before we can help guide them to an adjustment in the future.

SHOCK

No one is immune to shock. If the news of a parental separation or divorce is unexpected, it brings shock—to adults, to children alike. One is stunned, disbelieving. Lights flash, mind whirls, nothing is real. The universe spins, one's personal world shatters, and all learned rules no longer seem to exist.

In the midst of this numbness comes denial. "It can't be! This is a bad dream, a nightmare! Tell me it's not true!" And along with the denial come questions: "How did it happen? Why? Is there any hope that life can go back to the way it was?"

Tears eventually flow as the body digests what the mind has been told. In the ensuing hours and days, the person in this state cannot sleep; all interest in food disappears; parts of the body begin to ache; weariness and fatigue are constant with no relief.

Connie's seven-year-old son reacted to his parents' separation as if to a bad case of flu—body shaking and teeth chattering. He was "ill" for days and had recurrences for months. My three-year-old daughter sometimes acted as if in a coma—no visible reaction, just staring into space. I would go into the children's bedroom in the middle of the night to feed her baby brother and find my daughter sitting up in her bed, just staring straight ahead. She wasn't crying—just sitting stiffly, staring at nothing. Jeanne didn't register when I talked to her. And I couldn't seem to waken her; yet she wasn't asleep. Only holding and rocking her while singing softly would relax her body and mind and bring her back to consciousness. The "coma" reaction occurred again and again, always after falling asleep.

Following shock come other emotional stages, which are also universal: grief, guilt, feelings of rejection, unworthiness, inadequacy, and all types of personal fears. The reactions may come in sequence, out of sequence, together, separately, and continue for years. *The pain of bereavement is a state of slow healing.*

GRIEF

A popular children's author, Madeleine L'Engle, says *grief is like a deep cut—it doesn't hurt until the numbness wears off.*

Studies of children who have lost a parent indicate a pervasive state of sadness. When their minds accept the fact that something valuable has gone out of their lives, they mourn. I found this reaction common to the children interviewed on a local television show, *Children of Divorce.* Preschoolers who were asked, "How do you feel now that you're living with just your mommy (or daddy)?" would inevitably say, "I feel sad." Tears rolled down one little boy's face as he responded, "Bad. I feel bad. Won't my daddy ever come home again?"

Like us, *children express their pain in a variety of ways.* Most commonly, they cry. They may cry a lot, and even feel ashamed of their tears, but they shouldn't. Crying is one way of working out one's grief. It is a natural, human reaction. Scriptures tell us our Lord wept when he grieved.

Other manifestations of grief are similar to those of shock. Children may lose interest in playing, in their friends, in school. Kurt, Katie's six-year-old son, just seemed to mope around all the time. He didn't want to eat; he had trouble sleeping. Kurt tried to participate in family functions, but his heart wasn't in it. He was experiencing depression with all its gloominess, helplessness, and utter emptiness.

Some young people are terrified at being at the mercy of their own grief. Barbara's three teenagers were this way. They had spent so much of their growing time in learning to maintain control that they couldn't seem to recondition themselves. Like cats, they went off into separate corners of their private worlds to lick their wounds. They let no one in; they become lost in thought, in their own lost fantasies.

It was unusual for Barbara's three children to all react similarly to grief. Generally there are some differences. My older daughter was an eighth-grader when she sensed the problems in her parents' marriage. Two years later when the separation occurred, Jeanne had learned to accept it as fact. She turned mainly to her friends for solace and joy. The divorce brought her innumerable additional problems—personal problems, self-identity problems—which she talked about incessantly. She kept nothing in; everything was discussed again and again. She talked out her grief and sought counseling.

My son, on the other hand, kept everything in. He was in seventh grade when his father and I told him and his sisters we were separating. We all sat on the floor, my ex-mate and I quietly giving the news, the children asking questions—not many because the two younger ones were more or less in shock. Jon wept—but oh, so quietly. He kept his head down, and I remember thinking his body looked physically burdened, as if carrying a heavy backpack. His fourth-grade sister Jan cried more openly. She hugged us both, assuring us of her love.

I realized later that neither child totally accepted the news at the time. Oh, they accepted the separation, but they didn't really believe it would end in divorce. When that became obvious in the ensuing months, Jan cried openly upon its discussion, though she generally went immediately to her room for privacy. If Jon cried (and I'm sure he did), his sisters and I couldn't tell from his reaction. He did not like to discuss the divorce or any problem resulting from it. The mere mention of the subject turned this happy, talkative boy into a pained, silent one. He sat and listened, but gave no response. His reaction reminded me of his reactions to childhood illnesses. He had never complained or asked for the attention most children do. He just lay in bed, pain in his eyes, accepting the illness and living through it until recovery.

Reports from friends and acquaintances indicate that hyperactivity, fretfulness, anger, aggressiveness, losing emotional control at the slightest provocation are other expressions of children's grief. In some, grief is an "off and on again" affair, sometimes to the extent that one acquaintance wondered if there was a genuine lack of feeling on the part of his son toward his missing mother. But all these expressions of pain are not uncommon to children at this stage.

Doctors, counselors, clergy, anyone working in the behavioral sciences know that *grief produces pain, but the pain itself is really part of the healing.* The expression of pain shows that one is alive. The young child falls, skins a knee, and cries, but soon a scar forms, proving the body is healing. The adolescent in bed with stomach flu aches, regurgitates, and is feverish, but within hours or days the body recovers.

Grief is an expression of humanness which shouldn't be turned off or delayed. Children who attempt to deny their grief or try to bear it in silence are only postponing it. It is healthy to accept and express pain, and to work it through as part of healing. Eventually God "restores our souls"; he revives our drooping spirits.

GUILT

There isn't an adult who loses a mate in divorce or death who doesn't at some time or another feel guilt. *Children feel guilty too.* In talking to various young Christians, I found many who felt they were being punished by God for some personal sin, thus causing the departure of a mother or father. They may have had some secret resentment or anger toward the lost parent which they magnified into the sole cause of the loss. The guilt can run deep, so deep that many children have difficulty erasing their error in judgment. They cannot accept God's or their parents' forgiveness, although they have been assured again and again of the fact. Or they cannot forgive themselves.

In the case of divorce, *most children's guilt comes as the result of not knowing the facts.* When parents don't share the truth, children can only conclude they were somehow to blame. "My parents got divorced because I was bad," said Tommy. "I never obeyed. And I fought with my brother." Sandra's reason was, "I always left my radio on too loud. It drove my father crazy!" Another's reaction: "I wasn't good enough. I was selfish. I never helped my mom around the house." The reasons are endless, and all untrue.

Some children take guilt on themselves because they cannot believe their parents are at fault; they hold on to the belief that their parents are perfect. Needless blame and anxiety arise because the children have no answers or cannot accept the answers to the question, "Why?"

Young children especially are unequipped to handle situations over which they have no control, such as divorce. "But *why?*" says little Jordan in Marcia Newfield's *A Book for Jordan,* "Why can't we all stay together?" Like Jordan, many youngsters deny reality;

they want only for their parents to get back together again. Blaming themselves for their parents' divorce gives them a feeling of control over their parents' lives which they really don't have. If the fault is in the child, then the child reasons he or she can correct the fault and get the parents to marry each other again.

Another misguided way young Christians think they can accomplish the goal of reuniting a marriage is by striking a bargain with God. This is what a friend's daughter did. Unknown to him at the time, Jack's little girl promised God she'd never be "bad" again if he'd only make her mother come back to live with them. When her mother never returned, little Susan became devastated. She gave up on life—crying frequently—and only many sessions with her pastor and father brought her comfort.

Without plausible reasons for divorce, children often make up their own. They create logical explanations. My three-year-old assured me that her daddy would come home again if only I didn't make him eat that "awful green soup"—pea soup—which she hated. Connie's seven-year-old dreamed up the explanation that his parents had known each other only two days before getting married, and they should have known each other "at least a week." The older the children, the less likely they are to project fanciful reasons for their parents' breakup, but like their younger siblings, they want a reason—one they can accept.

REJECTION

Personal rejection is a natural reaction to the death of a parent or of a parent's marriage. It seems plausible enough in a divorce, but is even common in death. "If my father loved me," the child reasons, "why would he have died and left me?" And the child of divorce thinks, "My parents don't care about me at all. They only care about themselves."

Rejection brings with it feelings of unworthiness, of inadequacies. Children feel abandoned, unloved, unworthy of love.

37

Some children, like my son, withdraw into shells. Others look elsewhere to assuage the rejection. I had middle-grade students who focused on me, their teacher, for needed acceptance. One turned to her mother's date whom she felt would make everything up to her in the future. My teenage daughter was quite typical in trying to find the love she felt she had lost in a peer of the opposite sex. She convinced herself that this new relationship was real love, one which would not disappoint her as her parents had. She clung to the new love, rebelling against our parental concern over its influence.

Rejection is usually coupled with fear, and the most common fear children have is that of total abandonment. When young people are left with only one parent in the home, they become frightened that something will happen to the remaining parent and they'll be left totally alone. They want and need to know what would happen to them in such a case. Little Kurt was afraid that he'd have no place to live, that he'd be without food or clothing, that there'd be no one loving to take care of him if anything happened to Katie, his mother.

Barbara's teenage daughter didn't worry about being abandoned *now*. She was close to high school graduation and knew she could take care of herself. But Nancy worried about her future. She had self-doubts. "I feel inadequate; I can't relate to boys. If I wasn't good enough for Dad to be with me, how can I expect a husband to stay with me?"

Another fear children have is the lack of permanence. If their parents have battled over their custody in the past, they fear it will happen again—that they will be uprooted and placed into a new life-style. They have gone through one period of painful readjustment; they do not relish the thought of another.

And finally, children fear the loss of love from one or another parent. One girl interviewed on the television show mentioned earlier said, "I'm afraid of the time my parents actually sign the divorce papers. I'm afraid my dad won't love me or see me anymore. I'm afraid he'll remarry and forget me."

No matter what had happened between this girl's parents, no matter what she had heard one say about the other, she continued to love *both,* and she didn't want to lose the attention and support of her father. Like all children of single-parent families, she needed the assurance that both parents loved her. If their love seemed in question, the girl would be particularly susceptible to looking for a substitute elsewhere.

ANGER

Anger is one human response to not getting things the way we want them. It is as natural to children as to adults, and it happens in *all* families. In single-parent homes it is often the child's expression of protest—protest against the missing parent, protest against life. In divorce the anger may be directed against whatever parent is thought to be the initiator, or then again against the parent who caused the condition resulting in the action. In many cases both parents suffer from their children's angry protest.

Children through the age of twelve are inclined to take out their frustration and anger on siblings. Connie's seven- and ten-year-olds did. Bobby and Jimmy fought both verbally and physically with each other. They took each other's personal belongings, sometimes breaking them, and they often lied, each blaming the other for things he had done. Some of the students I had in school reacted to their parents' separation with antisocial behavior. Totally out of character, they turned into bullies, disrupting my classroom and their homes alike. Someone had to pay for the hurt and neglect they felt.

Unlike younger children, teenagers feel little sense of blame for the separation of their parents, but they also may react in resentment and anger. I haven't run into one yet who hasn't reasoned at one time or another that parents are *adults,* and as such they aren't supposed to *have* problems. Parents should have it "all together." If they can't work out their problems, they shouldn't expect a high school student to be the perfect child. This is an especially common rationale for the adolescents who succumb to the temptations always prevalent at their age—alcohol, drugs, sex, overindulgence of all kinds.

It is also not unusual for Christian children to turn their anger toward God. Jack's daughter Susan became despondent when she felt God hadn't answered her prayer, but other children become angry. "How much does God expect anyway? How can he be loving and still let this happen to me?" Doubts as to God's sincerity, his very existence, can arise. The children begin to look upon God as hateful, the initiator of their pain. When months pass and nothing seems to get better, they may become disinterested or even antagonistic toward worship. Their faith still exists, but it lies dormant in a cocoon. A long time may ensue before new spiritual life emerges.

In one degree or another, *children's anger can be turned inward.* Sometimes this results in exaggerated feelings of guilt, rejection, or unworthiness. Other times it manifests itself in withdrawal or in the embracing of everything "forbidden" and harmful, as if to punish one's body for the cause.

EMBARRASSMENT

At no stage of life are humans more susceptible to the opinions of their peers than in childhood. *Children are conformists.* They think and act as the group does. They have not lived long enough to know themselves, to understand that what's appropriate for another may not be right for them. They don't want to be "different." They don't want to be "left out."

A divorce in the family causes a frustrating, if not frightening, predicament for a child. The situation is awkward; it is humiliating. Children feel they no longer "belong." I was always glad that

40

Father's Day came after school ended for the summer so that my first-graders without a father at home didn't feel hurt or object to making a card for the absent parent. But it happened more than once on Mother's Day. And middle and upper-grade students often had no parent to represent them at a father/son or mother/daughter function. This caused them agonizing alienation and personal embarrassment. They were not "one of the crowd."

Children's embarrassment and fear of rejection are not without just cause. Both adults and children have stereotypes about divorce. Classmates and friends who learn the news can sometimes be very cruel, making fun of those from single-parent homes. They think the latter are now different or strange in some way, and their parents may want them to break off personal associations. Even teachers tend to discriminate, albeit subconsciously, against children of "broken homes," or to overprotect children whose parents are widowed—again, much to their embarrassment.

Thus some children react by hiding the fact that a mother or father is not at home. They don't allow their classmates to visit their homes for fear they'll learn the secret. They may even stop playing with their best friends. Yet as statistics indicate, there are *millions* of young people who are victims of the loss of a parent. There's hardly a classroom in the country where our children are alone in their situation, but often they are not aware of the fact. Too often a child in third grade does not learn until fifth that there were five, six, or more others experiencing the same loss and embarrassment as he or she was.

AGE REACTIONS

Although all children react to sudden death or divorce with shock, guilt, grief, rejection, anger, and embarrassment, there are responses that are more characteristic at one age than another.

Two- to four-year-olds often react by regressing in their development. They break their toilet training and revert to diapers. Katie's four-year-old Karen no longer wanted to feed herself. Instead she demanded to be fed as when she was a baby. Karen also let out her anger in destructive actions, such as throwing and breaking her toys. And she reverted to the two-year-old's favorite expression, "No!"

Four- to eight-year-olds may continue similar babyish matters, and often they allow their mothers to pamper them. I had a second-grader who simply gave in to his mother's overprotection. Gerald waited patiently after school until his mother appeared, took his coat off the hook, put it on him, and buttoned it up. She even put Gerald's boots on for him, a task he also was perfectly capable of doing himself.

Psychologists say that the most critical age for children of divorce is between the ages of six and eight, and statistics prove this is the one in which the largest number of children are affected. Children feel the loss of control in their lives the most at this age. In response they try to bring order out of chaos by reasonable explanations. Unlike Gerald, some youngsters assume responsibilities appropriate for adults or older children, becoming "little mothers" or "big brothers" to younger siblings. My neighbor's six-year-old decided to become the "man of the house." Randy tried in every way he could to make up for the problem situation in his family, even though he had both mother and older sister to lean on.

Eight- to twelve-year-olds react to the change in their lives more commonly with anger. They express their disgust and frustration in silent or visible protest. Connie said she was called in for school conferences regarding her ten-year-old Jimmy more often at this age than at any other. It is also at this time that many youngsters look for father or mother figures in friends' parents, teachers, or other adults.

Teenagers who blame anyone for a marriage breakup usually blame their parents, and they transfer their anger to one or the other. Much to their displeasure, they often find themselves the confidants of both mother and father, a role which is painful for them. This is a mistake we single parents make over and over— telling our older children *our* problems and our biased viewpoints regarding the reasons for our singlehood. The fact is that our children's loyalties usually remain with *both* parents, no matter what their actions, and they resent the dilemma of being caught in the middle if each parent tries to turn them against the other.

PARENTAL HELP

Parents can help ease children's grief, anxiety, and negative emotions caused by divorce or death by answering the three questions uppermost in children's minds:

1. How did this happen? What are the reasons?
2. Do you still love me? Does my father (mother) still love me?
3. How will my life be changed?

There is much evidence to indicate that *the brunt of the shock regarding divorce or death of parents can be lessened if children are given realistic facts.* Parents generally think young people are fragile in this regard and not capable of accepting painful realities. But most children are resilient, flexible enough to learn to cope and recuperate if they are guided from the beginning to understand what's happening.

Being honest with children also eliminates or decreases many of the anxieties they would otherwise face. It is difficult for young people to handle ignorance and parental furtiveness, for then fantasy runs free and their worst expectations can neither be confirmed or refuted. Truth, even painful truth, gives the child the security of knowing where he or she stands.

It is, in fact, futile to try to protect children from the realization of impending divorce or its causes. Most children have at the very minimum a vague sense of something being wrong. Wasn't this true of your children? Didn't they ever witness or overhear arguing between you and their other parent? Were they *totally* unaware of the coldness or apathy that may have existed between you? Did they ever ask for the reassurance, as 12-year-old Kevin, that "We *are* a happy family, aren't we?"

Though children may be aware that all is not right, they usually do not comprehend the pain their parents have experienced, and in some cases, of the years they have stayed together in a marriage "for the sake of the children." When the latter has happened, it is not unusual for young people in their teens or twenties to become upset with their parents later for having made this "sacrifice." Fred's college-age children reacted negatively on hearing this explanation. Instead of gratitude, they experienced guilt, a feeling that they were the cause of many unhappy years in their parents' lives.

But what exactly or how much should one tell one's children? Divorced parents lack objectivity when describing their marital life and ex-spouse, especially right after the separation, thus specific "sordid" details of parental conflict may better remain their private concern. Children will usually accept this, as they retain the right to certain privacies also. Yet vague generalities are not the answer. "It just didn't work out" has no credibility to a child who feels it is the adult's responsibility to make it work. "We stopped loving each other a long time ago" may be the truth, but it makes the child question the parents' continued love for him. That, however, should be dealt with when responding to the child's second basic question.

Connie, Barbara, Katie and I have pondered the answer as to how much to tell children regarding divorce, and we think it may be in the same measure as when they ask about sex at a young age: answer as much as necessary to satisfy their question, no less, no more. At any rate, that's how we handled it. As time went by some of our children asked for additional reasons or details, but as time went by we were also able to be more objective.

44

Although our answers differed, we all agreed that *children need to understand that they are not the cause of the divorce,* and to be assured that the way their parents feel about each other is not the way they feel about their children. Clear and definite statements of love must be repeated again and again. Whatever your explanation, it should end with, "But we have not stopped loving you. We will never stop loving you." And then you and your ex-mate must *prove* it in all your relations with your children.

In answering children's second query, *"Do you still love me?",* we parents must give an answer to the third, *"How will my life be changed?"* The main reason young people don't want a marriage to break up is because they feel more secure in it. Even if theirs is a less-than-healthy family life and they recognize it as such, the known present seems more comfortable than an unknown future. In this they are like many adults—the ones who will never risk the joy of fulfillment if it means making substantial changes. "Nothing ventured, nothing gained" is accepted only if minimal risk is involved. If adults choose to remain in limbo just because it's a "secure" limbo, little wonder that children have fears.

The truth is, *it's the periods of indecision in our lives that are the most difficult to live through.* We can procrastinate for years in deciding to make a move (professional, personal, whatever) and all the time we can't make up our minds, we suffer! Once we *make* a decision, however, the biggest battle is over. At that point we have some clear direction and can move ahead, not continue to tread water, a state of existence which is both unproductive and exhausting.

Thus before you can answer your children's third question, it is important that they understand the finality of your action. Because almost all children want to deny separation or divorce, children from toddlers to teenagers will try to get their parents back together until they accept divorce as reality. They may suffer needless anxiety and pain until they grasp the fact that nothing they

45

did caused the divorce, and nothing they can do will result in a remarriage.

Young people need to realize that their parents are divorcing each other, not them. Custody and visitation plans should be explained, and children's wishes taken into account. Youngsters want concrete reassurances that they will have a continued relationship with the noncustodial parent. Their lives should be disrupted and changed as little as possible.

A trip to your local library will produce numerous books you can use with your children to answer their security questions. These books were written specifically for children, or for children and parents together. They are only a few of the excellent "aids" that have been published and will continue to be published as divorce statistics rise. The juvenile fiction quoted throughout this chapter are examples of books your children can read independently. They are realistic, frank accounts of young people who have experienced, survived, and grown from the same situations in which ours are living.

CHILDREN'S READJUSTMENT

How long will it take for your children to readjust? It depends on their resiliency and ability to cope, and on how well you respond to their reactions and needs. Generally the initial impact dwindles away within a year or two. No matter how much time it takes, however, it is important to remember that like us, *children get worse before they get better!* The pain following surgery is often worse than the pain of the illness that caused it, but by the time the stitches are removed, the hurt has diminished and recovery begins. Thus even though the situation is painful and deteriorating at the time, it *will* improve, and sometimes very suddenly.

There have been many studies over the years regarding the results of divorce on children, and it would be folly to deny the impact and difficult period of readjustment. To quote the director of the Yale Child Study Center, "Divorce is *one* of the most serious and complex mental-health crisis facing children of the eighties."

I have read many case studies and case-study summaries on the effect divorce has on children, and the conclusions tend to be contradictory. The results "prove" the effects are either very bad or very good. They remind me of the old nursery rhyme:

There was a little girl
Who had a little curl
Right in the middle of her forehead.
And when she was good,
She was very, very good.
And when she was bad,
She was horrid!

Horrid. That's what some studies and many more headlines decide is the result of divorce on children. A national magazine which arrived this week titles the subject with "Woe Is One; Two Parents Are Better, It Seems." It quotes a study of about 8500 elementary and high school students from 15 schools around the country and notes that one-parent children showed substantially more absenteeism, truancy, discipline problems, suspensions, expulsions, and dropouts.

At first glance, that's quite a charge! However, there are some other factors to consider. First of all, 15 schools is not a very large sampling out of the 102,253 public and private schools in America, nor is 8500 students out of the 44,125,000 elementary and high school students enrolled during the early 1980s. But even if the results proved the same if *all* students were studied, it does not mean yours or mine would fall into this drastic category. Mine haven't; nor have the children of the friends and acquaintances I've discussed. All too often we single parents become too sensitive regarding negative reports we read. As a married friend said to me recently, "Kids with two parents have all kinds of problems too. Don't forget that!"

A close friend of mine who is a juvenile judge in Clinton, Iowa informs me that in almost all cases in which juveniles get into trouble, a study of the family indicates that one or both parents have serious problems of one kind or another whether they are single *or* married. I've checked this opinion with another friend, a court-appointed "referee" who makes recommendations to judges in Toledo's juvenile courts, and he concurs. These experiences support a recent study by a child psychologist who found that there was trouble between nearly all the parents of the disturbed children who were brought to her for help.

Many psychologists feel there is such a thing as *emotional divorce*—a marriage which is characterized by unhappiness, tension, and spoken or unspoken conflict. Research indicates that it is more of a strain on a child to live in an unhappy but intact home than in a single-parent home that is secure. The mere absence of that stress is healthy. Erasing the cause of the tension is a relief—a quiet, calming influence. My children, for example, have all decided they would not want to return to the conditions under which they previously lived. After living separately, they appreciate the absence of the "negatives" in their former family life.

Because we're all different, I don't place great faith in study conclusions regarding children of unhappy or divorced parents. I agree with the sociologist who answered the question "What is the impact of divorce on children?" with the answer "What is the color of birds?" Most studies don't really compare apples to apples, for no two "apples"—marriages, children within two-parent homes, divorces, children within single-parent homes—are the same. Besides, researchers don't study Christian families separately from others, and *a living, vital faith makes a big difference in one's adjustment*. Every Christian single parent I've questioned has attested to this fact.

Because there are no *irrefutable* research conclusions involving the effects of divorce on children, we should not let the negative opinions destroy us or become self-satisfied over the positive ones. The question is moot at this point anyway. Our children *are* living in single-parent homes. The point is, what are we going to do about it? We can never be sure if we did right or wrong by our children in the past. Either way we acted, the children would have suffered to some extent or another, sometimes without our ever being aware of it. In struggling over this dilemma, we have only one resort—to turn to God's mercy. Unless we accept Christ's forgiveness for this and all sins of commission and omission, we'll know little peace. And more important to our children, we'll be likely to remain too confused or guilty to be of any real help to them.

In helping our children, we might consider them in the light of the common emotions and reactions which they are experiencing. Would one or more of the following suggestions be helpful to their "healing"?

1. Ask your children if they understand what happened in your home—the causes of their parents' separation. Give them acceptable reasons. Try to be objective and truthful, neither building up nor tearing down their other parent.
2. Ask your children how they feel about their present situation. Discuss some of the common described reactions to see if they apply. Assure your youngsters that these reactions are normal and will dissipate in time.
3. Tell your children of your love and God's. Show it in your concern and actions.
4. Keep your children's lives as constant as possible. Find out in what ways they'd like you and their noncustodial parent to accomplish this.
5. Give each child time daily to just talk if he or she desires. Make sure they can count on that time and on your continued interest in their feelings and problems.

What do you need most in your new role as single parent? The assurance of God's *love*—"I have loved you with an everlasting love" (Jer. 31:3), and his *constancy*—"Jesus Christ is the same yesterday and today and for ever" (Heb. 13:8). Knowing this, you can transfer his love and constancy to your children. With God's and your help, their pain and sorrow will be replaced with peace and joy.

"Commit your way to the Lord; trust in him; and he will act" (Ps. 37:5).

4

Problems— The Doors to Opportunities

How are you going to do it all? How are you going to be: Mother? Father? Provider? Housekeeper? And who knows what else? All this, in your new state—alone?

YOUR PROBLEMS

You have to keep on working—or begin working. Financial responsibilities are there and will always be there.

And the children, with all their problems and readjustments, are with you. So you can't, and wouldn't want to, ignore their needs.

And the place in which you live needs caring for, too. The pantry needs to be stocked, the laundry done, the rooms cleaned, snow shoveled, lawn cut, and on and on.

And you're all alone. Or so it seems.

But you're not. Never. Your Lord is always with you. "He will not fail you or forsake you" (Deut. 31:6).

What resources does your Lord give you? Well, for one thing, he gives you yourself. It doesn't seem like much right now. You, with all your own insecurities, frustrations, weaknesses. It's too overpowering at times. You break down under the pressure of it all; you cry, you waste time feeling sorry for yourself; sometimes you just give up.

But you're no weaker than anyone else who's lived. And you have no more problems. Paul felt the same way you did over the responsibilities placed on him. Moses found excuses to avoid the task God demanded. Jonah tried to flee God's command. And Abraham was asked to sacrifice his only son, Isaac. Even our Lord in Gethsemane prayed, "Father, if thou art willing, remove this cup from me: nevertheless, not my will, but thine, be done" (Luke 22:42).

And in the end, the Father knew best. He knew what all these people could take—could *do*—with his help. One by one, they abided by his will, accepted the challenge, and succeeded! And so can you. You can know, like Paul, "I can do all things in him who strengthens me!" (Phil. 4:13).

YOUR RESOURCES

So what are your resources again? God! First of all, and most importantly, God. With him you can do anything. *Anything* . . .

And secondly, yourself. God working through you.

And perhaps God has also given you support groups—a parent, a sibling, a friend, an understanding employer. Oh, there are all kinds of people God has given us to help us, if we only look around and search a bit.

But even without support groups, God has given you another resource you may have not considered—your children. Yes, your *children!*

"How easier it would be," you might be tempted to think at times, "if I didn't have all the responsibility of the children. Single life might be far simpler to adjust to."

Would it really? Oh, you could immerse yourself in your work or in your social life. It would work for a time. But someday you'd realize you're doing everything just to escape the fact that you were all alone. Someday you'd miss one of the greatest blessings God can give us—our children.

So forget that line of thinking. Your children are nothing but a blessing. They are not the "problem" at all. They are the reward! There is no sacrifice you'll make at this point of your life that you will regret at any point later. God is asking no sacrifice of you; he is only giving you an opportunity.

YOUR SOLUTIONS

Our Lord tells us to consider the wisdom of the world at times. He says, "Be wise as serpents" (Matt. 10:16). That does not have a negative connotation, but a positive one. What has life taught you about the act of living? How have people from time immemorial learned to live in a world of problems? How do they survive? How do they prosper?

Use the wisdom God has given you for a moment and consider your single parenthood in an objective, "worldly" way. Displace all your emotional reactions and entanglements and look at your life on the basis of common sense. Think facts, only facts. Pretend this is not a "human" problem, but a "material" problem—a thing that is something you can tackle on a truly objective basis.

Few of us have degrees in business. But if we were in business school today, what we would learn boils down to four important aspects. We would learn to 1) *analyze the situation,* 2) *list the problems,* 3) *decide how to turn the problems into opportunities,* and, 4) *make and follow an action plan.*

It makes sense. And God has given you sense. If you believe in "God the Father Almighty, Maker of heaven and earth," the opening words of the Apostles' Creed, then consider Luther's explanation of these words:

I believe that God has created me and all that exists; that he has given me and still sustains my body and soul, all my limbs and senses, my reason and all the faculties of my mind. . . .

And so, using your "reason and all the faculties" of your mind, consider the advice of business. First of all, write down a situation analysis of your present life. Let's take a hypothetical case for an example:

SITUATION ANALYSIS

- I am a Christian woman: have been one all my life.
- I was married and now am divorced.
- I have three children.
- They are ages 5, 11, 17.
- They have never known a home without their father.
- And I have never been a single parent before.

So fine, that's your situation. It wasn't so difficult to write. You knew all that anyway. "Now comes the hard part," you think. Let's see. What are the "problems" related to the situation described above?

PROBLEMS

- My children feel (see descriptions in Chapter 3) about their new single-parent family.
- My children miss their mother (father) and I can't seem to make it up to them.
- My children seem to resent me (and perhaps life).
- My children don't obey me.
- I feel inadequate to meet my new responsibilities as single parent.
- I don't feel well; am exhausted all the time.
- Pressures at work are building; my job is very demanding.
- There aren't enough hours in the day to fulfill both my job and home responsibilities.

- I can't seem to balance my budget.
- My ex-mate and I are barely on speaking terms (or has died).

These are just a few of the problems the single parent encounters. Yours may differ. If you don't have one or another of the problems listed, consider yourself fortunate. For all the problems you put on your list, you could have more, or more drastic ones.

And what about opportunities? Well, some of them were already described in the situation analysis.

OPPORTUNITIES

- I am a Christian; my children are too. Ours is a Christian home, with Christ and his church as support.
- I have the additional support groups of family, friends, neighbors.
- I have myself, my own "reason," my abilities, resources, job.
- I have my children, with all the talents and abilities God has given them.

In addition, you have other "opportunities."

- Time heals; life may get worse for a while, but eventually it will get better; readjustment always takes time.
- I love my children and they love me.
- My children are part of this new single-parent home. They are partners with me far more now than they were in the past.
- As partners, my children can share in the planning, working, and life-style of our new situation.
- In sharing in the planning and working, my children and I have the opportunity to communicate, really communicate, perhaps for the last time in our lives.
- In communicating our true feelings and personal problems, my children and I can learn to know each other better, to see what emotions and drives make each one tick.

- In learning to know each other better, we can learn to accept each other's faults, to respond to each other's needs, and to comfort and support each other.
- In loving each other, we can in turn be loved for ourselves, be comforted, and supported.
- My children can grow in love, strength, and independence, more able to meet whatever successes and disappointments their future brings.
- And so can I.

No matter how long a list of problems you can make, the list of opportunities will be longer. Your single-family life has the opportunity to demonstrate what living in Christ, the abundant life, is all about.

But the opportunities are nothing—merely words—without an action plan. None of them come about by themselves. Many people, even Christians, spend their whole lives immersed in their situations, their problems. They never find out who they are or what solutions and enrichment God offers them. They wait for "something to happen," for God or a loved one to step in and make everything all right. They run *from* the problem instead of *to* it.

You can't afford to run. You can't afford a missed opportunity. If there is any good that God can offer you out of your present "bad" situation, it's this growth.

Situation Analysis, Problems, Opportunities, Action Plans— once learned, you can apply these simple steps to all facets of your life at any time. You will be able to take any strand of your life separately and analyze it.

In future chapters, you will see suggested action plans for family living, family discipline, relationships to old and new parent-partners in the family, and the like. They are similar in their goals, but differ in their actions, just as your goals are similar to other Christian single-parent families, but your actions differ depending on you and your children.

For now, concentrate on your situation. Record and study the three steps suggested here as they apply to your life. Take your time. Involve your older children in the task. Don't look for solutions yet; they depend on careful analysis of your own problems and opportunities.

What does God the Creator promise you? What has he given you? Read the remainder of Luther's explanation of the First Article below. Rejoice over the reference to family. Be thankful that God has not tested your faith as he did Abraham, but that he has *proven* his love in the sacrifice of his own Son. He *is* with you, your loving Father always . . .

He provides me with food and clothing, home and family, daily work, and all I need from day to day. God also protects me in time of danger and guards me from every evil.

All this he does out of fatherly and divine goodness and mercy, though I do not deserve it. Therefore I surely ought to thank and praise, serve and obey him. This is most certainly true.

5

All for One,
and One for All

The date was December 25, 1978. I inscribed the book "Psst! Sometimes I think there's a Bubba and Babba in this house, and their initials are J.A.N. and J.O.N. Love, Mom."

THE WORK TO BE DONE

So true. The book—*Bubba and Babba,* by Maria Polushkin—is based on a Russian folktale. It tells the story of two lazy bears who were always arguing over household chores. One day they disagreed as to who should wash the dinner dishes. Bubba had chopped the wood for the fire and reasoned that it was harder work than Babba's cooking of the meal. But Babba contended that *everyone* knows a cook never has to clean up afterwards. Finally Bubba had a "brilliant" idea. The bears would simply *leave* the dirty dishes, and whoever was the first one to get up the next morning and the first to speak would have to wash them.

You can imagine what happened. Both bears "slept in" all day and neither let out one peep. At first it was fun, but as the day wore on, Bubba and Babba found it tiring to feign sleep, and their enjoyment wore thin. Yet stubbornly, neither would give in. It was only Raccoon's unexpected visit that resolved the situation.

There's a bit of Bubba and Babba in all of us. If we could, we'd much prefer to let someone else do the tasks we don't like to do. We might even exert energy "tricking" others to doing our work for us. But we're not all Tom Sawyers, and our family members don't think fence whitewashing is any more fun than we do. So usually we single parents become the Little Red Hen and do all the tasks ourselves.

Thus we often find ourselves on a treadmill, trying to meet everyone's needs alone where two did before. Without a doubt, single parenting can be absolutely exhausting! We feel exactly like Alice in Wonderland as she raced along with the Red Queen:

> And still the Queen cried, "Faster! Faster!" and dragged her along. "Are we nearly there?" Alice managed to pant out at last.

> "Nearly there!" the Queen repeated, "Why, we passed it ten miles ago! Faster!" And they ran on for a time. . . .

> "Now! Now!" cried the Queen. "Faster! Faster!" And they went so fast that at last they seemed to skim through the air, hardly touching the ground with their feet.

And what's the result of all our efforts? We race and race and race, and when we finally stop to rest, we find ourselves exactly at the place from which we started. We protest as Alice:

> "Why, I do believe we've been under this tree the whole time! Everything's just as it was!"

> "Of course it is," said the Queen. "What would you have it?"

> "Well, in *our* country," said Alice, "You'd generally get to somewhere else—if you ran very fast for a long time as we have been doing."

"A slow sort of country!" said the Queen. "Now, here, you see, it takes all the running you can do, just to keep in the same place. If you want to get somewhere else, you must run at least twice as fast as that!"

This excerpt is from Alice's adventures *Through the Looking Glass,* and a more apt title couldn't be found. We look through a looking glass of household tasks, do them, look back again, and see the same jobs to be done once more. And frankly, right now, we are unequal to the task. It takes all the running we can do, just to keep in the same place. We know we can't run twice as fast as that. There has to be another answer.

WAYS OF DOING THE WORK

Katie and Connie ran their races alone valiantly—and lost. They tried to be "Super Moms," doing everything for their children, but they never got everything done. Katie finally gave up on it all and put the sign "Chicken Little Was Right!" in her kitchen. Connie didn't go that far, but she admitted the sky had almost fallen down for her.

What had Barbara and I done? We simply expanded on something we learned as children. We expanded on something we had carried out in married life. *We let our children share in household responsibilities.*

No doubt you had similar work experiences as a child. Did you find it so unusual to be assigned tasks even though your mother didn't work outside the home? If she was like mine, she spent more hours on church and charitable work than some of us do on paying jobs. Or perhaps your mother had a larger family, or fewer conveniences to assist her than you and I do. And so we kids chipped in. We cleaned our rooms; we cooked; we did the dishes; we ran errands. We helped. And we were no worse for wear. We learned from it!

EGALITARIAN LIVING

Today this kind of family living is called "egalitarian" living. In two-parent families egalitarian living usually means sharing—talents, abilities, workloads. It means proportionate giving, proportional living, to everyone's benefit.

In single-parent families, egalitarian living is often all this, plus more. It's akin to its dictionary definition: "Equal rights for all citizens." The children don't have absolute "equal rights," of course, but then equal rights are never the issue in Christian living. Two adults, after all, will often give up their rights on this or that point for the benefit of the other.

What *is* important in egalitarian living in single-parent homes is equality in communication. *Each member of the family has a voice, a right of expression.* Even without the final say, that means a great deal. My daughter Jan remarked to me the other day that I *listen,* really listen, to her more now than I did when she had two parents. Happily married people are inclined to talk and listen to each other more than to their children.

Egalitarian living is advisable in any home, but in the single-parent family, it is a must. Without a spouse partner, single parents need a partnership relation to their children. That does not mean they "unload" on their children, force too mature responsibilities on them, or in any way use their children to compensate for a mate. What it means is that they include their children in the decisions that affect them all.

PERSONAL ACTION PLAN

Before incorporating egalitarian living in their families, single parents have to take stock of *themselves* first, going through a personal analysis as described in the previous chapter. Katie and Connie both said they had to set down initial action plans for themselves before they could proceed with ones for their children.

61

Until they did that, they continued to race with the Red Queen, getting nowhere but close to exhaustion.

Personal action plans may call for some reorientation. *We single parents have to learn where we are* now, *not where we* were. We have to face facts. We have to disregard stereotypes about super moms and dads. We may have to reject well-meaning, but bad advice from friends who have never lived our experiences. There's an old Indian proverb that says never to judge someone until you've walked in their moccasins. We do well, therefore, to follow the examples of other single parents who have learned these lessons from years of raising children alone:

1. Don't try to be both parents. Don't try to compensate for the missing parent. Be either your children's mother or their father; you can't be both.
2. Try to involve the absent parent in parenting as much as possible. (More on this in Chapter 7.)
3. Be yourself. If you don't you won't be able to live with yourself, and frankly, neither will your children.
4. Be honest with your children.
5. Involve your children with household responsibilities.
6. Set up your own family priorities for living.

Note the first point. *Almost every single parent falls into the trap of trying to compensate for the absence of the other.* "My poor son has no father," a neighbor said to me, "I must make it up to him." And so she began trying to do the impossible, engaging in football every Saturday afternoon, a sport for which she had no interest or ability, simply because her son and his father had done so in the past.

Other parents try to overprotect their children. Jack concluded his older daughter could no longer walk to her music lessons, he had to drive her there. He spent every available minute with Kristen, leaving her no time to pursue personal interests. Yet he couldn't understand why she resented all his well-intended attention.

Jack learned what many of us learn the hard way—that when we try to be *both* parents to compensate for our children's loss, we may put an added burden on them. Our actions could imply that our children should try to be everything to us also. And hard though it is for us to replace the missing parent in their lives, it is harder for them to replace that same person in ours. They are wholly inadequate for the task.

Barbara feels it's equally imperative for us to be ourselves. "To thine own self be true," she quotes from *Hamlet*. After a long, hard day's work, for example, Barbara never had the patience to listen to her children's school problems until after she'd eaten. So she was honest about it. She told her children that most workdays left her exhausted in mind and body, and until she ate and rested she was of little use to anyone. Her children understood. Because Barbara was *herself* and honest with her children, they were able to be *themselves* and honest with her.

Being honest is always good advice. Children see through us anyway, so we're only fooling ourselves when we pretend to be anything but ourselves. Think back to your own childhood. You knew when your parents were conning you—or themselves—and when they were being truthful.

I've been honest about family expenses with my children as they've grown older. The budget notebook of recorded bills sits on my desk, and the children log in food and personal expenses as they occur. I think it's important that they can track annual increases in electric bills, for example, so they understand when I ask that they conserve energy. My father always told me to turn off the lights when I left a room, but I never actually saw what electricity cost the family. You may have to explain that a child can no longer have a personal telephone if that is the case, or demonstrate why waste in food or other commodities is so costly. If your family action plan will involve children's participating in rebudgeting on a limited income, they'll need to know something about it before you ask their input in helping you make financial decisions.

The fifth point in your orientation may or may not be new to you: "Involve your children with household responsibilities." As stated previously, this is really nothing new in family living. Many a child in generations past heard Paul's advice to the adult Thessalonians applied to him: "If any one will not work, let him not eat" (2 Thess. 3:10).

All children benefit by assisting in the home. A toddler can help set the table and give the baby her bottle. A primary school child can clean much of his room, sweep the steps, cut out cookies, sort clothes. By fifth grade, many youngsters are capable of more responsible household duties. I learned to cook when I was ten, for example, and as each of my children reached this age, they learned too. They cooked one meal a week, planning the menus under their father's and my supervision. The latter was especially important in the case of my son, for his first meals were generally casserole and potatoes—his favorite foods. The rest of us were not as enchanted with all those carbohydrates, however; thus the result was a lesson in nutrition and diet.

All these "assists" can be done, are done, or will be done in two-parent families also, especially as more and more women join the work force. Only 13% of all American families are the old "traditional" model with a father as sole breadwinner and a mother who has no job outside the home. Statistics also indicate that people are living singly longer before marrying than previously. Thus it's important for both sons and daughters to learn how to do various household tasks independently. How many men do you know who first learned to cook after divorce? How many learned the hard way that colored clothes don't mix well in hot water with whites? How many women had to learn how to repair things around their homes after they became widows? How many first learned how to change a tire when they had no man to do it for them? *Male/female roles don't apply to single life!* Singles have to learn everything—do everything—themselves!

There's no way we can predict how much of our children's lives will be lived singly. Thus following an egalitarian living pattern now will not only be beneficial to us, but to our children—now and in the future. After studying the situation analysis of where we are and where we want to be in this new life-style, we must make a decision about family priorities.

FAMILY PRIORITIES AND DUTIES

We need a family priority action plan. If we have any children who are old enough to have friends and activities outside the home, we need to plan family priorities. Without them, communication will break down. Mary Ann will forget it's her night to pick up the milk from the store because she was playing at a friend's, and dinner will be late while someone makes the trip, or it will be too late and there'll be no milk. Tom will work an unscheduled night at the drugstore and leave his dinner cleanup duties without a backward glance, necessitating us or a sibling to take over his responsibility. Without a priority list for egalitarian living, there will always be conflict, with family members deciding on their own what takes priority for what occasion.

What is a sensible, workable, set of time priorities if everyone in our family is to participate for the good of all? For my family, it is the following four steps, in the order as numbered.

1. School
2. Family duties
3. Job outside the home for older children
4. Social life

Schoolwork is first in the child's list of responsibilities. School is to the child what our jobs are to us. It must be taken seriously; no excuse must be made to put it elsewhere on the list.

Family duties come next in a child's priority of time. If they don't come next, they won't come anywhere. When a family jointly assigns a task to a family member, the person assigned must not think that he can do this or that job when it suits him or if he has nothing better to do.

There will be exceptions to this second priority, of course. Illness is one example. Other exceptions will be at the child's request. A birthday party may require a younger child to trade jobs with a sibling or with us, or to request permission to do it earlier or later than scheduled. A chance to work some extra hours at the neighborhood gas station may do the same for a teenager. But the point is, the child should understand that he or she wants the exception and should take personal responsibility for someone to cover the assigned tasks at home.

The third priority applies mainly to teenagers. Working outside the home is good experience for them. It helps them learn responsibility under another set of rules, and trains them for their adult working life. It also gives them pocket money (which they always need) and money for college or other worthwhile expenses. Even younger children can get paying jobs elsewhere—baby-sitting, for example, or delivering papers, shoveling snow, and the like.

And finally, there's the child's social life. It may be last in a series of priorities, but it is very important nonetheless. No person, child or adult, should have to live a life devoid of socializing. Reverting back to the Puritan mindset that all fun was sinful *is* almost sinful. "All work and no play" truly does "make Jack a dull boy." Healthy emotional growth involves relating with friends and enjoying the positive pleasures God offers us.

Whatever your list of family priorities, there will always be exceptions. When they are requested, you will have the final responsibility in the decisions, based on your children's reasons and feelings. If there's no one else available to take over the work missed, you probably will have to do it, but it won't be as difficult or as exhausting as before because you've let all the children help you in the overall task.

FAMILY COUNCILS

One way to set egalitarian living and family priorities in action is to use family councils. In preparation for a family council, write down your family priorities and a list of the duties around your house. Then call a family council. You will have family councils regarding other matters also, but limit this one to a family action plan for egalitarian living. The session may not take long, or it may take over an hour; it's not the length that is important, but the results.

Remember that *the purpose of this family council is to explain the fact that your children are partners with you and you'll be running the family together.* One way you can demonstrate this fact is by the seating arrangement you and your children assume during the session. Think about the last time your employer called you in to talk. Did he or she sit behind a desk and you in front of it? If so, was there any question in your mind as to who possessed the authority? Have you ever had a group discussion in which everyone sat around a round table? How was that more indicative of equality than when one person faced all others?

Seating arrangements are important to family gatherings in which everyone is encouraged to voice personal opinions. My children and I sometimes sit in a circle on the floor. A round table is excellent, but even a rectangular one will work if you have a child sit next to you rather than your sitting alone at one end. If you prefer to sit in living room chairs, however, don't make yours the "Papa Bear's chair," as Connie's sons call it. Avoid having a light on next to your chair, wherever it is. Whenever talking to children, singly or in a group, it's better to sit in a shadow— a darker area than they—if you want your children to relax and tell you what's really on their minds.

When your family gathers, explain the purpose of the gathering. Describe egalitarian living in words appropriate to your children's ages. *Assure them of your love and of your openness to their viewpoints.* Make sure they understand that every member has an equal voice in expressing him or herself (oldest *and* youngest).

Then explain that you:

1. Are not going to try to be both parents to your children.
2. Will try to involve the missing parent in their lives as much as possible.
3. Will be honest with them about your anxieties and problems and want them to be also.
4. Have a list of household duties and want them to help decide how to divide them among family members.
5. Have a set of priorities for family members' time.

Go back to the situation analysis, problems, and opportunities of this new family life-style (see previous chapter) and discuss them simply and truthfully. Explain that the purpose of this meeting is to develop an action plan for family living. Barbara's children picked up the new terminology and found it challenging. Connie's offspring just sat there, not responding. They weren't used to family discussions; their parents had made all decisions for them before.

Don't be disappointed if your first family council "doesn't take." Many a first session has long periods of silence. Even my children weren't too impressed. They felt they had heard all this before, so what else was new? For us, future sessions got better; the children opened up more and more. If this happens to you also, don't hurry the communication process. Don't do what we're all tempted to do: make up for silence by constantly talking ourselves. Children will consider this just another adult lecture, just another adult kidding him or herself that children count in decision making.

If your children have doubts about your motives, you will have to prove that you want them to have a voice in what goes on in your household. It may take some time with group gatherings and private talks. Obviously if you have difficulty showing love or interest in other aspects of your children's lives, they'll find it difficult to respond to your new proposal too.

But if nothing else, you can propose family-time priorities and set up a tentative schedule of individual duties at this first council. Explain the reasons for your order of priorities and see if your children have others, and for what reasons. Read the entire list of household tasks and let everyone respond to what they prefer to do or not to do. Let them make exchanges with each other and you. Let *them* make the decisions whenever possible.

One last subject for your first family council. Put a church priority in as a given. Normally time spent there will not conflict with school or home, but raise it as an issue. And if you haven't already, teach your children to set apart a portion of their income (allowances, job, gifts, etc.) for the Lord's work.

FAMILY FOLLOW-UP

After your family council, type or write the following lists:

1. Family priority list
2. Master plan of all duties listed under names of family members responsible, or under days of the week with duties and names responsible
3. Individual lists of duties for each family member

Put the priority and master duty lists on the refrigerator, family bulletin board, or any other place accessible to everyone. Give the other lists to the appropriate family members.

Try out the family priority list for a few weeks, listing exceptions and/or problems it causes. Discuss it at a later council and make adaptations if necessary.

Reconsider the master duty list after a month, and involve the entire family in making any necessary changes. Repeat the process at the beginning of summer vacation, a new school year, when a child gets (or changes) a job, or for similar reasons. Children—like all of us—tire of some household tasks and appreciate switching. In so doing, they also add to their experiences preparatory for adult life.

In executing family action plans, we have to remember that we do not own our children. Children are a gift from God that must not be misused. I have a poster in my laundry room that says, "Love people, use things." I've known more than one young person who became exhausted from trying to balance an academic program with meeting the needs of his or her parent(s) and younger siblings. We have to guard against expecting too much too soon. The opportunity for duties to change throughout the year as needed for any child's benefit is an important part of our action plans.

RESULTS

Respect is a cornerstone of egalitarian living. One of the greatest gifts my parents gave to me as a young person growing up was their *respect* for me. After love, I can think of nothing that impressed me more. My parents never tried to live my life, or make personal decisions, *for* me. They respected the judgment God had given me, and encouraged me to use it wisely. When parents respect their children, a good relationship develops. Children are inclined to live up to their parents' respect and that, in turn, produces more. The cycle continues, and everyone wins.

Children whose single parents have involved them in equal living usually respond positively. Sharon was a shy person until her father encouraged her to open up and declare her feelings about home life. He took what she had to say seriously. The experience made Sharon more self-confident, more assured in all aspects of her life. She was justifiably proud of her transformation and of the contributions she made to her household.

Brian became his family's supermarket wizard, scanning ads and coupons and making wise decisions that earned him a family "budget champion" award. His sister followed her younger brother's interest and began purchasing her clothes out of season or on sale. She saved herself money, but remarked that her family members' new relationship saved her in more ways than I could imagine—ways more profitable than financial savings.

"At first I wasn't very keen on the idea," said Scott, "but then I realized we needed to give Mom a break. She needed free time too. We really don't have that much more to do under the new plan. And it's made a big change in Mom!" "I do my own thing, I figure Mom should have time to do hers too," said another teenager. "Besides, she's a lot more livable that way."

I have a dear friend who's conscious of all the responsibilities I have in raising children alone, tell me, "Be good to yourself, Alice." That's what's beautiful about egalitarian living. *Everyone is good to each other.* In so doing, we're good to ourselves. "Let us love one another; for love is of God, and he who loves is born of God and knows God" (1 John 4:7). How well John's advice applies to us 19 centuries later. How well it will *always* apply.

"As the Father has loved me, so have I loved you; abide in my love. . . . Love one another as I have loved you" (John 15:9, 12).

6

Spare the Rod
and Spoil the Child?

Speak roughly to your little boy,
And beat him when he sneezes:
He only does it to annoy,
Because he knows it teases.

So sang the Duchess in *Alice in Wonderland* as she nursed her
child. As the result of this continual "loving" care, the baby
turned into a pig, and Alice was quite relieved to see it trot away
quietly into the woods. "If it had grown up," she said to herself,
"it would have made a dreadfully ugly child; but it makes rather
a handsome pig, I think."

DISCIPLINE: DEFINITION AND HISTORY

Discipline. What is it anyway? According to my unabridged dictionary, the first definition of discipline is *"Training that is expected to produce a specified character or pattern of behavior,
especially that which is expected to produce moral or mental improvement."*

72

The second definition is *"Controlled behavior resulting from such training."*

What do most people equate discipline with? The fifth definition: "Punishment intended to correct or train."

Equating discipline with punishment is nothing new. An ancient Chinese lad, for example, who carelessly made a blot on his writing tablet was forced to drink a dish of ink. If his hand got into mischief, he received a sharp and agonizing whack over his palm. An old Egyptian proverb states that "A boy's ears are on his back, and he hears only when he is beaten." Hebrew synagogue schools followed the Proverbs: "Do not withhold discipline from a child; if you beat him with a rod, he will not die" (Prov. 23:13).

During the Middle Ages, discipline was also severe. Monks had been taught that the body was the enemy of the soul, and it was to be punished. At one German monastery, all the boys were whipped regularly once a month, just to be on the safe side. At an abbey in England they were all flogged on Christmas Eve in order to make Christmas Day "sweeter." In Thomaschule, where Bach taught, each failure to obey a regulation resulted in some form of punishment. The rules were many, from "failing to close the door when last to leave" to "being sick enough to vomit in the wrong place."

The famous *New England Primer* used in the American colonies includes this verse of discipline:

GOOD CHILDREN MUST

Fear God all day,	Love Christ alway,
Parents obey,	In secret pray,
No false thing say,	Mind little play,
By no sin stray,	Make no delay,

In doing good.

A major part of a teacher's job was to keep discipline. He had, after all, between twenty and a hundred pupils of varying ages crowded into a room thirty feet square. A rule helped him keep unruly knuckles in line, and a "gad" (lithe five-foot hickory sapling) could reach even the farthest sinners without his having to leave his high desk and stool.

In the 19th century the birch rod still remained in American classrooms, and many a Tom Sawyer felt the proverb, "Folly is bound up in the heart of a child, but the rod of discipline drives it far from him" (Prov. 22:15). In addition, whisperers had bits put in their mouths; restless squirmers had horses' blinders strapped to their temples; children who talked impertinently were forced to eat soap. Poor Tom Sawyer was both whipped and shamed for being tardy—"Now go sit with the girls, and let this be a lesson to you!"

Way back in the 11th century, however, the theologian Anselm wrote that in training youth, "we should learn a lesson from artists, who do not fashion their gold and silver images with blows alone, but press and touch them lightly, and finally complete their work with gentleness." In the 15th century Gerson, chancellor at the University of Paris, recommended a mild discipline in his *Bringing Children to Christ:* "Above all, let a teacher try to be a father to his pupils. Let him never be angry with them. Let him always be simple in his instruction, and relate to his pupils that which is wholesome and agreeable."

Martin Luther suffered unduly harsh discipline at home and school during his childhood and advocated the "true way to bring up children" is by "kindness, and with delight. . . . For what must only be forced with rods and blows will have no good result, and at farthest under such treatment, they will remain godly no longer than the rod descends upon their backs." He spoke against those who use:

> passionate violence in bringing up their children. Such dis-
> cipline begets in the child's mind, which is yet tender, a

state of fear . . . and develops a feeling of hate toward his parents, so that it often runs away from home. What hope can we have for a child that hates and distrusts its parents?

GOAL: SELF-DISCIPLINE

If discipline *is* "training to produce a specific pattern of behavior," where did you and I get our *training* to train our children? Nowhere, probably. In most cases, we received no training. So what do we do? We discipline our children the same way our parents disciplined us—right or wrong. Or, if we didn't like the way our parents disciplined us, we take just the opposite stance—right or wrong. Or we follow the advice of our children's other parent. Or we just ignore the whole thing and follow no pattern at all— giving in one time, spanking another, trying to "buy" our children's obedience in one way or another, and the like.

Perhaps the main reason we vacillate in our means of "training" is because we never think of the overall goal based on the second definition of discipline: "controlled behavior resulting from such training." That sounds good, but controlled behavior *when?* Just when we're around? Or always?

"Always!" responds every parent I've asked. "I can't be with my children every hour and day of their lives. I want them to be disciplined all the time—even when I'm not there." If that is true, then what we're really after for our children is self-discipline:

"Training and control of oneself and one's conduct, usually for personal improvement."

Self-discipline involves freedom of choice. If I'm in control of my discipline, I must make choices: I can do this; I can do that. But there are ramifications of every act I do or not do. I can choose to pay for the groceries I collect at a supermarket, or I can choose to walk out without paying for them. But if I choose the latter, I've broken a law of society, and I'm likely to pay the consequence. If I break a traffic law and run a red light, the ramifications of my nondiscipline may not only hurt me, but it could bring physical injury to others. And if it does, the punishment will be harsher than if I had taken groceries without paying. Society makes laws. But the choice to follow them or not is ours. Nobody makes the choice for us.

It's the same way with child self-discipline. When you as a parent make rules for life and family living that you feel are good training to produce a God-pleasing pattern of behavior in your children, then you expect that these rules will be followed for the good of the child and everyone else in the family. But there are only two ways you can guarantee the expected outcome. First, you can follow your children around day and night and make sure. However, that's as impossible as a police officer following you around every minute to make sure you follow society's laws. It isn't going to happen; it's not possible. So your alternative is to train your children to follow the rules independently. The goal for our children is to teach them *self-discipline.*

EXAMPLES: SELF-DISCIPLINE

I had my first lesson on how to train children in self-discipline at a parent-teacher meeting a long time ago. The school hall was crowded with parents asking questions about discipline to the guest speaker, a child psychologist. Here are some they asked:

1. What do I do with my sixth-grade daughter who refuses to eat all her dinner? I cook a well-balanced meal; she eats only what she likes. A few hours later she's hungry again, and so she snacks.

2. My preschooler never picks up his toys after he plays. The toys are strewn all over the living room. I've shown him how to put them away; I've even helped him; but usually he walks away when I tell him to pick them up, and I do all the work.

3. My fourth-grader never does his homework. He goes out to play unless I catch him. After dinner he wants to watch TV. I have to nag him every night to do his homework.
4. My teenager never obeys my curfew. He always comes in late, no matter how much I harp about it.
5. My kindergarten daughter plays with matches. We've told her again and again how dangerous it is, but she keeps lighting them in the basement. She could burn down the whole house, let alone burn herself terribly.

The complaints went on and on. Parents had been nagging and scolding, but nothing seemed to work.

The child psychologist advised first of all to *stop all the nagging and scolding.* How did we react to lectures when we were children? We "turned off," didn't we? So do our children. They simply tune parents off, wait until they calm down, and then continue their usual behavior. Parents rarely do more than rant and rave anyway.

"Stop all the threats and nagging," the psychologist directed. "Instead explain what your rules are, and what will happen if they are not followed. Then put the choices to the child. He or she can follow the rules or cannot. It's up to them. But if they do not, they must realize and accept the ramifications of their choices. And after explaining and giving the child one or more chances to 'forget' (depending upon the age), explain once more and then follow through."

The follow-through was emphasized because without it, nothing would change. Let's look at some of the psychologist's responses to the discipline problems offered.

The girl who wouldn't eat all her dinner yet snacked later in the evening was to be told it was dinner or nothing—no later snacks. She could choose to eat her dinner, or she could choose to go to her room and remain there without the benefit of TV or other entertainment until the next meal—breakfast the next morning. The choice was hers.

The preschooler who wouldn't pick up his toys and put them back into the toybox after playing was to be told the toys were his total responsibility. He could take them out of the box and play, but if he did so, he was to put them back again afterwards. If he put them back, he could keep on playing with them. If he didn't, the toys would be packed away. The parent was to put the toys out of sight for a day, two days, a week, depending upon the situation. When the child asked for them back, he was to be told why they were gone and they wouldn't come back until he promised to put them away after playing. When the child asked and expressed understanding of the conditions for getting them back, the toys were to be returned. If the child forgot again, the same measures were to occur—no spanking, no yelling, just firm action until the discipline of putting the toys away became automatic self-discipline.

The fourth-grader who preferred to play rather than do homework was to learn that play was a privilege that came after work was done. His friends became off-limits—totally! So did TV. Both were to be restored once the self-discipline of doing assigned schoolwork was established.

The teenager who always came home a half-hour late in the evening with a different excuse every time was to find no excuse counted. The next time he was late, he wouldn't be allowed to go out at all for a week. He'd find it embarrassing to admit to his friends that he was being disciplined. He'd learn to enact the self-discipline of coming in on time because it was more face-saving then to admit discipline was enforced upon him.

And what about the little girl who played with matches? Should her parents hide them all? The psychologist said no. There was a time for spanking—a harsher method of "training"—and that time was when children had been told repeatedly that what they were doing was harmful for them (or others) and they continued doing it.

There are occasions, he said, when a whack accomplishes what weeks of patient explanation and restraint have failed to do. When a child repeatedly runs out into traffic, hits a younger sibling, purposely causes damage to objects not belonging to him, then a determined, "I said no, and I mean it!" accompanied by a spanking may be the only helpful deterrent. It is not unlike the lesson a young child learns when after being warned not to reach up and touch the top of the kitchen range does so anyway. One day the heat is on, and the child's hand is burned. The child learns quickly and painfully that he or she made the wrong choice, and it's unlikely the child will ever repeat the action. *Self*-discipline will be the child's deterrent.

CHILD INTENT

Why a child does a negative action is a very important factor in disciplining. I once punished a newly-transferred second-grader in my class for cheating. He had to stay after school and redo an assignment, this time *not* copying his neighbor's paper. In talking to him later, I realized he had never heard of the concept of cheating. It seemed unbelievable, but it was true. He was genuinely perplexed over my disciplinary measure. The first-graders at his former school had copied others' work without question from the teacher. He had not realized he was doing something unacceptable.

I had similar experiences at home. During each of my children's preschool years, I entered the living room to find them scrubbing down upholstered furniture with cleansing powder. Each time I was dismayed! The children had witnessed me using the same cleanser to scrub sinks and thought they would help mommy by using it to scrub furniture. They weren't punished, but they got an explanation of why that was unacceptable behavior.

Intent is not always evident. That's why communication is so important. Why did the child do or not do this or that? What reasons might there be that we can't ever imagine? And if the child had legitimate or understandable reasons, we should reconsider. We should ask forgiveness for any disciplinary action we take in haste and later regret—even scolding. When we're wrong, we should admit it. Our children will understand that. They will, in fact, respect us more if we admit we are as human as they.

Sometimes a child who normally "behaves" does something totally out of character. The infringement may be major or minor, and we can't imagine what possessed them to do it. When I went to elementary school, we took our lunches if we stayed over the noon hour. After Easter we all brought Easter eggs and our own salt shakers. One day during second-grade lunch period, I took the top off my plastic salt shaker and slowly poured the salt onto the floor next to my desk. If my teacher hadn't seen me do it, she would never have believed it; believe me, she was dumbfounded. As a matter of fact, so was I.

Dear Mrs. Zettel stood next to my desk and asked why I had done such a thing. I really didn't know how to answer her. I had no logical reason. It just seemed to be the thing to do at the time. It was dumb, but I couldn't use that for an excuse. And it wasn't particularly fun. I just did it. To this day, I'm not sure why. I simply remember being fascinated watching the salt pour in a steady white flow onto the floor. And then suddenly there was this mound of salt on the floor and 40 kids yelling, "Teacher! Look what Alice did!" I was never punished for this act. I guess this loving woman had learned much from her many years of teaching, and I loved and respected her all the more for understanding what I did not.

BIBLICAL DIRECTIVES

If ever we single parents miss a mate, it's when we have family disciplinary problems. There's no one to ask advice of, no one to take over when we've exhausted our resources. We all want fast answers. We all want instant results. Why can't our children immediately follow St. Paul's dictate: "Children, obey your parents in everything, for this pleases the Lord" (Col. 3:20)? Whatever happened to the Fourth Commandment: "Honor your father and your mother" (Exod. 20:12)?

The Bible speaks of the rod and the law of punishment in the Old Testament, and of kindness and the law of love in the New Testament. Perhaps Hebraic parents were inclined to be over-lenient with their children and thus needed stern instructions. If so, they wouldn't be different from parents of all eras. Luther wrote that many "knowingly neglect their children and let them grow up without proper instruction, bringing about their ruin; and though they do not set a bad example, yet they spoil their children by undue indulgence. . . . Such false love blinds parents so that they regard the body of their child more than his soul. Hence the wise man says, 'He who spares the rod hates his son; but he who loves him is diligent to discipline him' " (Prov. 13:24).

How could Luther say on the one hand that children will "remain godly no longer than the rod descends upon their backs," and on the other hand agree with the proverb quoted above? Perhaps the answer lies in the RSV translation of Proverbs 19:18: "Discipline your son while there is hope; do not set your heart on his destruction," or in Luther's explanation of "Fathers, provoke not your children to wrath, lest they be discouraged" (Col. 3:21):

Yet St. Paul does not mean that we should not punish children, but that we should punish them from love, seeking not to cool our anger, but to make them better.

"To cool our anger." How many times were we punished as children to cool our parents' anger? How many times have we punished our children to cool ours? How often do we really discipline "from love . . . to make them better"?

PRACTICES AND STUDIES

Professional studies and writings by trained child counselors attest to the fact that *many children have never actually been taught to obey. Thus they are apathetic to rules and authority.* Interestingly enough, this is not because their parents are neglectful, indifferent individuals who fail to take their parenting responsibility seriously. Often they are the products of a general revulsion against the severe discipline of the Victorian era. In addition, a misunderstanding of John Dewey's educational theories has convinced many adults that children should be allowed free expression and restraint from the imposing of behavioral limits or their future emotional and mental health will be endangered. Popular periodicals have even proclaimed that a well-behaved child might indicate a cruel and dominating parent.

"Spoiling"—permissiveness—was not a factor in child discipline during the early years of our century, however. In 1928 John B. Watson wrote advice on child rearing which included:

- Don't spoil your babies by picking them up every time they cry.
- Don't allow thumb sucking.
- Feed babies according to a fixed schedule whether they are hungry or not.
- Toilet train babies within the first year.
- Treat young children as though they were young adults. Never hug them or let them sit on your lap. Never kiss them. If you must, kiss them once on the forehead when they say goodnight. Shake hands with them in the morning. Give them a pat on the head if they have made an extraordinary good job of a difficult task.

If parents did all this, said Watson, they'd become perfectly objective and "utterly ashamed of the mawkish, sentimental way [they] had been handling" their children in the past.

In the 1940s Dr. Benjamin Spock began a trend towards more permissive and flexible child-care methods. Parents were advised to follow their own common sense and adapt schedules to fit both the child's and their own needs. Interestingly enough, the pendulum now appears to be swinging back to the "moderate degree of control, firm discipline, and punishment when necessary" suggested by Walters and Grusec in 1977 as a positive approach to child-rearing.

In discussing children's reactions to divorce in Chapter 3, I said that they are basically resilient and will adjust in time. That children have flourished under the wide variety of rearing methods used throughout the centuries is yet another indication of their adaptability. *It may also indicate that specific methods are less important than the basic attitude of parents.*

During the late 1960s and early 1970s Baumrind made an intensive study of the effect parents' behavior have on their children. Children who were the most confident and self-reliant had parents who were warm, loving, respectful of their children's opinions, and yet generally firm and clear about the behavior they expected. Children who were fairly self-controlled and self-reliant, but not very secure and somewhat withdrawn and distrustful, had parents who were either very or fairly controlling, but more concerned with their own needs and not very affectionate toward their children or concerned with their opinions. The parents of the most immature children were warm towards their children, but not very demanding. These permissive parents, who neither rewarded responsible behavior, produced children with the least self-reliance and self-control. *The study concluded that competence and self-confidence in children was best fostered in warm, nurturant homes where parents reward responsible behavior, yet also encourage independent actions and decisions.*

PARENTAL RISKS

If our children are to become confident, self-reliant, and self-disciplined, we'll have to be definite as to what behavior we expect

83

from them. Children need limits. They need to know the rules; they need to know where they stand. They need to have a sense of consistency and order in their lives.

Many of us don't lay down a pattern of rules and order that will lead to self-discipline because we don't want to take the risk of making our children unhappy. We like to have disciplined children, but we don't feel we have the right to expect children to accede to our wishes. We single parents, especially, often have the mistaken idea that human rights apply only to our children. We don't want to cause more grief, more tears, more frustration. We don't want our children to hate us. We hope that discipline will somehow come about by itself, with no verbal, sullen, or tearful protest from our children.

But learning is learned. It doesn't come about by itself. The most effective learning is that which comes from experience, but much of it is frustrating or even painful. Although we are afraid to frustrate our children by teaching them self-discipline because along the way we may evoke their displeasure, we did not hesitate teaching them to walk, and that involved many a fall before they mastered the act. We watched them learn to skate or ride a bicycle, and we simply smiled when they tumbled, only to pick themselves up and try again. Frustration is often unavoidable in learning, but it's not necessarily harmful.

Respecting one's children is as important in instilling self-discipline as it is in egalitarian living. And it involves taking risks. When my older daughter was a high school freshman, she asked if she could go to a party instead of Maundy Thursday services. It wasn't that Jeanne disrespected worship; she planned to attend Good Friday, Holy Saturday, and Easter Sunday services. But it really bothered me. It seemed very disrespectful to go to a party on that night.

I knew the appeal. The party was to be held in an elegant Lake Shore Drive apartment building with its inviting social room overlooking Lake Michigan. I didn't approve of the attendees: they seemed a little wild to me, and the supervising parents a bit too sophisticated. But I decided to take a risk. I told Jeanne that my parents had respected my judgment in high school, and I would hers. I went on and on, setting up the choice to go or not to go in such a way that there was no possible choice at all. And after I got all through with this obvious verbal conditioning against attending, I asked her what she was going to do.

"I'm going to the party," Jeanne said.

"You're *going?*" I asked increduously.

"Yes," she said matter-of-factly, "I'm going."

Well, what could I do then? After all that talk about respecting her judgment, never dreaming it would differ from mine, I couldn't go back on my word. That was one of the first times it became clear to me how different generations are, and what a risk we take when we allow young people to walk in their own moccasins along paths foreign to us.

I spent that evening not unlike King Darius who had allowed Daniel to be thrown into the den of lions. I suspected there would be pot smoked at that party, and perhaps more dangerous drugs would be used. I wondered if my daughter would survive the peril.

The next day I asked Jeanne how the party went, and she said, "I don't know. I wasn't at the party very long when the hostess' mother asked me to come to the apartment." It seems one of the girls had arrived under the influence of drugs, and soon "flipped out," according to my daughter. She and Jeanne were only acquaintances, but it was Jeanne she called for when she was hurting. And what did she want from my daughter? She wanted to known why Jeanne was different, why she wasn't a "burnout," why she believed in Christ. So Jeanne spent the remaining hours of the evening testifying to our Lord's love and influence in her life and of his love for this girl also. Jeanne recounted this to me as matter-of-factly as she had when she said, "I'm going." Apparently it was not a new experience for her. I didn't understand her culture, but she did. And she had learned to live within it and still remain a child of God.

CHILD RESPONSIBILITY

Instilling self-discipline involves training our children, and then trusting them to live up to the training. "Train up a child in the way he should go, and when he is old he will not depart from it" says Proverbs 22:6. But throughout the process *it is important that young people realize they are responsible for their own behavior.* When Katie's sixth-grader got into trouble at school, she excused herself by saying someone else had put her up to it. Katie got out the Bible, read the story of the Fall in Genesis, and asked Karen how God reacted when Eve said the serpent had put her up to it.

Sometimes it takes children a while to realize that nothing or nobody else causes them to misbehave, that in the long run we are all responsible for our own actions. When my son entered high school, he had no friends there and soon fell into a group of five young men who found it great fun "cruising around in a car and doing dumb things," according to Jon. For four months he participated, happy to belong, but finally he realized he really didn't enjoy spending his time this way, plus there was the threat that the "dumb things" could become dangerous activities. Yet he didn't want to lose the only friends he had, or felt he had, at the time. Unknown to me, he struggled with this dilemma until finally he decided to tell the others what he thought of the activity, even at the cost of losing them as friends. It was at this point he informed me of the risk and asked my reactions. I discussed the "trade-off" aspects and said what he already realized: it was his decision. He decided to tell his friends how he felt, and to his amazement, he found that three of the five agreed with him. Nobody wanted to be "different," so everyone conformed. And if they got into trouble, they reasoned, at least it wouldn't be any one person's fault.

Yet even though children are liable for their behavior, there are parents all over the United States who feel *they* are totally responsible. Centers have sprung up in Manhattan, Minneapolis, Seattle, Boston, and other large cities to help parents who can no longer handle the guilt regarding their children's negative conduct. And single parents feel a double guilt. But parents are usually responsible only if they have done nothing to teach their children self-discipline. And even then, they may fail. Children differ. "Parents do have a tremendous effect on their kids, but kids are also born with personalities that affect their behavior. . . . Genetic factors and home environment are not the sole influences on how children turn out," say Alexander Thomas and Stella Chase, psychiatrists. "Parents need to learn to put responsibility for actions where it belongs—on the youngster," a Families Anonymous representative says. If your children have exceptional problems, seek professional help—for them *and* for you. Too often parents suffer from child abuse—in one of many ways or another.

CHILD DIFFERENCES

Children are all different. They even differ within families. Do you recall the parable Christ told in Matthew 21:28-31? One day a father told his first son to go work in the father's vineyard. The son said, "I will not." So the father told his second son to do the same work. The second son said, "I go, sir." So far it looks like a typical family—one son disobeyed, one obeyed. Ah, but the first son did *not* disobey. He said he wouldn't do as his father asked, but then he thought better of it. "Afterward he repented, and went." The second son, on the other hand—the one who immediately voiced his consent—"went not."

How many children are like the first son? They object to unexpected assigned tasks. They verbalize their disapproval and insist they won't do it. But they *do* do it. And then there's the opposite child—the kind that says yes only to placate a parent, but then does as he or she pleases.

Why are there differences—sometime striking differences—between children? Why do similar parents have children who turn out so differently? Why do parents who are quite different have children who act similarly? And why won't one set of rules work for all children? Or one method of training?

Psychologists have studied human behavior for centuries and proclaimed various "reasons" based on genetics, environment, culture, and the like. But the fact is there is no common conclusion. Children simply *are* different, and we're not totally sure why. And because they are, we have to respond to each one as an individual.

Doing this means we may have to adjust the rules differently for each child. We do it matter-of-factly with regard to their ages. "Why can Tim stay out till midnight and I have to be in at nine?" asks a younger sibling, for example. Basically we have one set of rules in our training program, but we do make adjustments from child to child.

PARENTAL HELP

Frustration in learning self-discipline can be lessened if we parents make our directions clear. If we are to teach children our standards it's important to set down what is and what is not permitted.

Along with a well-defined set of rules and directions, children need encouragement. Too often, however, they receive discouragement instead. "Criticizing children," notes Dr. William Glasser, a Los Angeles child psychiatrist, "is the worst thing you can do, because it's not objective, not something the child can handle. It's too full of emotions." Another psychologist, Dr. Dan Kiley, warns, "Never hit a child on the mouth or anywhere on the face. Children have told me that, when slapped on the face, they feel as if they've been insulted, not punished. The face can be viewed as the gateway to the soul."

Fortunately, punishment is rarely needed if children are given positive rewards. Punishment only tells children what they have done wrong, and excessive punishment may result in anger, revenge, and a sense of endless failure. On the other hand, verbal praise and encouragement are usually more effective.

Remember what happened when your toddler took his first step? He received your encouragement. He fell, perhaps started to whimper, but then stopped when he heard your words of praise. He was cheered on, so he tried again. You expected him to fall; you would have never considered scolding him for it. He had to learn from the fall. Children have to learn from their mistakes. And they'll make mistakes in obedience. They'll fall too, but finding out that doing certain behavior pleases the people they want to please will make them try to remember to always behave that way.

Children turn a deaf ear to criticism, but never to praise! Praise gives them a positive self-image. Putting down children makes them feel stupid and inept. Comparing them with siblings or friends' children who do better may make them so unsure or terrified of failing that they'll give up and won't try at all. Or they'll turn positive energies into negative actions and compound the discipline problems. *Children have an uncanny way of living up—or down—to what is expected of them.* Barbara and I have teenagers who respect our concern over their comings and goings and who show it by keeping us informed. When I returned home from work late the other night, I found this note from my 14-year-old:

Dear Mom,
I went out with Lisa, Rosanne, Jeanette, Joe and Kenny. All their numbers are in the book, I'll be home between 9:30-10:00. Maybe earlier.

Love you! !
Jan

Family councils are helpful for meeting disciplinary problems that affect the whole family. In discussing the problems with your children, give an analysis of what's happening to upset the positive dynamics within family relations. Encourage everyone to talk. Don't cut off any youngster's point of view, but encourage constructive criticism among family members. Anger has no place in a family council. If we have a Christ-centered home, then our Lord is in the midst of all our actions. We cannot afford to tell him to stand in the corner while we thrash out our differences. We'll want to follow our Lord's example of being fair, honest, and compassionate. When siblings learn the reasons for each other's actions, they usually are understanding and forgiving.

It's often more effective in fostering a confidential, trusting relationship to talk to an individual child alone. Perhaps the only reason a child is misbehaving is because he or she feels neglected. *It is so easy for us to neglect to "listen" to our children.*

This is the message in a book by a friend of mine, Florence Parry Heide, called *The Shrinking of Treehorn*. In it, little Treehorn begins to shrink one day. He's worried, so he tells his mother as she's baking a cake. She responds by saying that's too bad, looking into the oven, and expressing the hope that her cake won't fall. By dinner Treehorn has shrunk so much he can hardly see up to the table, but his father contends "Nobody shrinks" when Treehorn points up his dilemma. The next day at school he is sent to the principal, who doesn't listen any more than anyone else and is alarmed that Treehorn might be "shirking." Treehorn finally finds a way to regain his original stature, no thanks to the grown-ups who couldn't be bothered with his special problem, but that same evening he looks in a mirror and notices he's turning green. Treehorn decides not to tell anyone. "If I don't say anything, they won't notice," he rationalizes. How sad, but how true far too often.

The more children we have, the more work we have, the less we listen to our children. The other evening I was writing very late at night when my daughter called from college. She had nothing particularly pressing to talk about, she just wanted to talk. As the minutes ticked by and the "small talk" continued, I found myself becoming impatient and wanting to get back to my written train of thought. Then the irony of the situation hit me. I wanted to stop listening to my daughter so I could continue writing a book about how to raise children.

Not that children should be able to interrupt us or siblings no matter what we are doing at the time. "I'm busy, but I'll give you time later," is a very acceptable way of handling such a request. As long as the child knows he or she can count on our time and knows that we'll follow through, then our response will be accepted. But just as there are times when we say, "I want this behavior to stop, and NOW!", there are times when our children say, "I want to talk to you, and NOW!" And when it is that important to them, then nothing should be more important to us.

Basic advice on discipline for children can be summarized in a few words: *Be consistent. Be firm. Be in control. Give specific clear directions. Give choices. Follow through on corrective measures. Show respect.*

The most obvious advice and child need is often ignored, however: *Give love.* Some of us find it difficult to demonstrate affection. About the only way we are able to do so is to smile or to give a word or two of praise. But our children need more. No matter how much they seem not to care, they need a physical hug, a caress, an arm around the shoulder. They might draw away, but they are moved when we make the move.

So then, "make love your aim" (1 Cor. 14:1a)—by a loving embrace, by a special smile, by an encouraging remark, by a listening ear, by an approving tone of voice, by a gentle touch, by a patient acceptance of the child's ideas, by daily prayers.

This chapter began with the Duchess' lullaby—a very negative lullaby regarding child training. But Lewis Carroll, the author of *Alice in Wonderland,* wrote this lullaby as a parody on a well-known English poem of his day entitled "Speak Gently." Its first verse is a more fitting ending to a discussion of child discipline.

Speak gently! It is better far
To rule by love than fear;
Speak gently; let no harsh words mar
The good we might do here!

7

Yes, but
I Have Custody . . .

Falling in love. Is there any experience quite like it? No one, nothing, is closer to us than our loved one. And everything is perfect.

WHATEVER HAPPENED TO THAT LOVE WE HAD?

When I was in high school I read John Greenleaf Whittier's poem "Maud Muller" in American literature class. I thought it was so sad. Maud, a "simple beauty with rustic health" was raking hay in the meadow one day when she glanced up and saw the Judge riding "slowly down the lane, smoothing his horse's chestnut mane," and Maud and the Judge, of two different worlds, fell in love. Both fantasized what joy it would be to be married to the other, but then the Judge "thought of his sisters, proud and cold, and his mother, vain of her rank and gold. So closing his heart, the Judge rode on, and Maud was left in the field alone."

The Judge "wedded a wife of richest dower, who lived for fashion as he for power," while Maud's simple husband eve after eve "sat by the chimney lug, dozing and grumbling o'er pipe and mug." Yet the Judge and Maud never forgot each other:

> Oft when the wine in his glass was red,
> He longed for the wayside well instead.
> And the proud man sighed, with a secret pain,
> "Ah, that I were free again!"

And Maud thought of him:

> A manly form at her side she saw,
> And joy was duty, and love was law.

Whittier concluded his poem with the oft-quoted lines:

> God pity them both! and pity us all,
> Who vainly the dreams of youth recall;
> For of all sad words of tongue or pen
> The saddest are these: "It might have been!"

We Americans are romantics; we believe in romantic love. We usually have the good fortune to marry the person we choose, the person we love. And if by some chance we cannot, we continue to remember the person with fondness and a special, tender ache the rest of our lives. No matter that we love someone new, some little incident can trigger the old feeling.

Single parents. Whatever happened to the love we had when we were first married? What went wrong? We thought it would never end. Other loves might end, but not ours. It was too real. It would grow better with age, like a fine wine.

But it didn't. Once upon a time we loved our mate so totally we were assured we'd live "happily ever after." But for many of us what began so beautifully ended so bitterly—so painfully. The person who knew us best—who knew us through and through—is now gone. We feel that person "left" us, literally or within the marriage. One way or another we feel deserted, or rejected.

HOW WE FEEL NOW

When we are first separated or divorced, we cannot look at ourselves objectively. We cannot understand why our marriage failed or what part we may have contributed to the failure. All we know is the feeling of being betrayed, abandoned, rejected. As a result we are angry and resentful. Some of our anger is connected with fear. We wonder what's going to happen to us. We don't seem to count with our ex-mate anymore; can we ever count with ourselves or someone else? We're confused; we're depressed; we're afraid! And our fear makes us angry. It's too early to turn the anger on ourselves, so we turn it on our ex-spouse. Deep down we may realize we are not perfect, but we don't have the courage to delve into our inner psyche and confront it. So we shut out such introspection and blame our ex-mate for our unhappiness. And sometimes we continue to do this for years.

Oh, we know all too well how *we* feel. The thing we can't understand is how our children's *other* parent feels. All we see is anger and irritation similar to ours, and we surely can't understand that. Who is *he* or *she* to be upset? *We* are the ones now left to our own resources. *We* are the ones with all the responsibility. We are the single parents who must carry on the raising of the children alone in addition to putting our lives back together again. We have at least twice the troubles the other parent has.

But we have the children. *We have the children!* Think for a moment what our lives would be without them. The first chapter of 1 Samuel records the life of Hannah, a woman who *didn't* have children. Hannah was one of two wives. She had to share her husband Elkanah with another *wife,* a situation most of us would find difficult enough. Yet in addition, Hannah was barren while her rival Peninnah had many sons and daughters, a fact which she used to taunt and to ridicule Hannah.

Now it is sad enough today when a woman wants children as badly as Hannah did and cannot bear them, but in her day it was not only a personal tragedy but a humiliating condition. This was a society in which a woman's worth was measured by her ability to bear many children. She had little enough social standing with them, but without them she had *nothing*—she was a failure.

95

God eventually blessed Hannah and she bore a son. But Hannah could love and care for little Samuel only until he was weaned, for then she fulfilled her vow and took the boy to Eli and a life of service in the temple. Hannah would continue to love her child, but Samuel would be apart from her. She'd see him only once a year, on the annual trip to Shiloh.

I was reminded of Hannah by a single father who told me he felt very much like her on losing his young son in divorce. "I'm thankful I can see Timmy once a week rather than only once a year like Hannah," he said. "He's the only thing that keeps me going." Sometimes having our children is the only thing that keeps *us* going.

HOW OUR EX-MATE FEELS

Grief—the grief you and I have experienced in the loss of a marriage—is extensive, but it is not compounded by the loss of our children. There are so many things in life that remind us of the difficulties caused by our single-parent status—TV commercials, for example, in which happy two-parent families are discussing breakfast foods, or buying a car, or sharing shampoo. But we don't know what it's like, as the father of my two young children told me years ago, to see babies or children of any age flash across the screen and be so overcome with grief that it's necessary to turn off the TV. Noncustodial parents suffer the depression of being "divorced" from their children as well as from their spouse.

Grief, fear, rejection, loneliness, all the emotional reactions we've experienced as new single parents are not exclusive to us; our ex-mates also know them intimately. They, too, weep, become hysterical, lose the ability to concentrate, feel weighed down by a sense of failure. We see how they react to us, and we remember most vividly the negative reactions, but usually we don't see or care to see *why*. "I blow up at her almost every time I visit the kids," said one father. "I vow I won't the next time. She's a good mother, she has it rough. But every time I get to the house, she hangs a guilt trip on me. She doesn't have to say a word: one look from her will do, and I instinctively seethe in anger."

Most of us do not know exactly what our ex-spouses feel. If we enjoy a good communication relationship with them, we are so appreciative we don't take the chance of spoiling it by putting old feelings and problems under the microscope of analysis. If our friends enter the single-parent experience, we usually learn only one side of the story—the side of the friend in the marriage who was closest to us, or the one who experienced a similar set of conditions.

I have friends who can't understand why, for example, their ex-mates suddenly indulge their children with various gifts, food, and costly expeditions which they considered extravagant in the past. "What's happened to Judy?" asked Jack. "She's an intelligent woman; she knows what makes kids tick; she never spoiled the children when we were married; why is she spoiling them now? The children chatter on and on about the wonderful things 'mommy' does with them, and they play with their seemingly endless new toys with great delight."

I understand Jack's frustration and veiled jealousy. I had similar emotions when Jeanne and Jon chattered on and on as young children after an exciting day with their father. They only wanted to share their fun with me, but I could take just so much talk about their good times without showing my resentment. I was remarried, but it didn't make any difference.

So my children, young as they were, simply "clammed up." When I asked what had happened, if they had a good time, they'd answer noncommittally, "Oh, nothing much. Yah, it was fun." I put a wedge between my children and myself by not being able to handle the fact they could enjoy their father's company unless I received the same oral "strokes" about their being with me. I didn't understand *their* feelings, let alone his.

97

Sometimes noncustodial parents admittedly overindulge their children. One father told me he didn't have much time with his youngsters, but what he had, he wanted them to enjoy *spectacularly*. "Before I was divorced I took Michael to the park and sometimes bought him a box of Cracker Jacks or a balloon. Now I take him only on expensive outings and buy him things he didn't even ask for." Perhaps one day soon his son will ask that he quit taking him someplace "special" each week and instead just play a game of catch. This is what 10-year-old Jeffrey does in Rose Blue's *A Month of Sundays,* a book pointing up the strain on children when parents act differently towards them after divorce.

The profusion of material gifts noncustodial parents present to their children are often a cry for acceptance. The parent gives the child a gift, hoping in return the child will give him or her the gift of love. Little Karen said, "Daddy gave me this bunny rabbit to hug and kiss good night because he can't do that any more when I go to bed." So Karen hugs that stuffed rabbit until she falls asleep. Like all children in single-parent families, she wants the security of knowing the absent parent loves her.

We're not so different. If we didn't have our children living with us, we'd want the same assurance. Emotionally and physically isolated from our youngsters, we'd want the security of knowing they remember us and continue to love us. And we might try to gain this in ways we'd never consider if they were living with us.

Another way some noncustodial parents seemingly change their personalities or behavior is by suddenly showing no interest in their children. It doesn't appear to make any sense, particularly when couples were married 20 years or longer and the now absent parent was always involved in the children's lives. Why, suddenly, should they retreat and rarely, if ever, contact their children?

Sometimes the reason is that of Barbara's ex-mate. Phil said he was confused, guilty, still "finding himself." He missed his children, yet he was afraid he had done emotional damage to his offspring and thought they were better off without him until he could show the strength and direction in their lives that he had in the past.

Another noncustodial father explained similar behavior in a different way. "Seeing my children points up my loneliness even more than not seeing them. I come home to a dreary apartment and it's so quiet! The bleak walls scream, 'You're alone! You're all alone now! Everything you had is gone!' But when I go visit my kids, I feel even lonelier. The house is full of sounds and action, the kitchen smells of the foods I love, the children's hugs and shouts of joy at seeing me are so sincere. You'd think I'd bask in it all—if only for the moment. But I can't. I just can't. Maybe in the future, but not yet."

Stepping out of our role as custodial parent to "role-play" the role of the noncustodial parent can help us understand and begin to accept all the actions or nonactions that so frustrate and irritate us now. In 90% of all divorce cases, custody is awarded to the mother (though prior to the 20th century, just the opposite was true). Yet the continued closeness of the father to his children is of primary importance to the youngsters and to their adjustment. We noted in Chapter 3 that it was healthy to try to involve the absent parent in parenting as much as possible. Children who fare best are those who are able to maintain full and loving relationships with both mother and father.

HOW OUR CHILDREN FEEL

Children not only *need* both mother and father, they *want* both mother and father. It's a rare child who does not want to see his noncustodial parent. This only happens if that parent rejects the child, or the child feels rejection. But generally it is *our* feeling of rejection that stands in the way of our children's healthy growth. We resent the other parent or disapprove of his or her actions and thus consciously or subconsciously deter the association with the children. As Connie's mother told her, "*You* chose

Bill as your children's father. You may be bitter about his actions to you, but remember, he's the only father your children have. They need to be able to love him."

In Chapter 3 we discussed the emotional stages children go through after the loss of a parent. The three questions uppermost in their minds are:

1. How did this happen? What are the reasons?
2. Do you still love me? Does my father (mother) still love me?
3. How will my life be changed?

The best way to answer the second question is to let the other parent have the opportunity to tell and prove his or her love. *We should not stand in the way of our ex-mate's legal right and God's command to them to remain the best parent possible.* When we do, we not only threaten our youngsters' needed love for that parent, but we jeopardize their love for us. As one young man so vividly put it: "Mom breaks her neck to keep Dad from seeing us. Man, it's always something. There's a battle every weekend. She can't understand that we love him and we want to see him. She acts so selfish and just plain dumb. I'd go live with Dad if I could."

A teenager answered how her life had changed by saying, "Not much. Dad's work makes him travel, so we never saw much of him except on weekends anyway. Now we still do. He's wonderful; he's still so involved with us. I guess that makes Mom wonderful too because she isn't like other divorced moms. She doesn't give Dad any hassle. She's just happy if we're happy."

Those are some words of praise. They're words we'd all like to hear. The girl thought both her father and mother were wonderful. She knew her absent parent loved her because of his continued involvement; she knew her mother loved her because she put the daughter's needs above her own personal reactions. Because the girl's life hadn't changed any more than necessary, she could work through the adjustment period quickly and with little pain.

BITTERSWEET SINNING   65714

Recently Connie was helping her son learn the Ten Commandments, and after Jimmy went to bed she called me to discuss the Eighth: "You shall not bear false witness against your neighbor." "Boy, that hit me," she said. "I kept expecting Jimmy to equate 'neighbor' with 'ex-husband,' because he sure could have put together a case against me. I've been putting Bill down for years." Connie's fear was that in trying to destroy her husband's reputation with her son, she may have unknowingly destroyed a necessary part of her *son*—his need to love and trust his father.

Even more "delicious" than telling faults, however, are verbal outbursts of anger. We've all experienced the tension that so easily flares into anger between ex-mates. Every one of the children interviewed on the TV show *Children of Divorce* testified to it.

Little Becky was three when her parents separated, and five when they divorced. She remembers they fought "for a long, long time" [two years], but I didn't know why [it was over the settlement]. I kept saying, 'Stop fighting! Don't yell at my mother!' " Her mother testified that Becky would interrupt their arguments to tell each parent "I love you" over and over, tearfully. A four-year-old boy turned to his mother on TV and said, "I feel sad. You two fight. You two always fight." A teenage girl said, "I'm sick of it! I don't know what the issues are, and I don't care! I just wish you two would quit the fighting!"

Barbara's daughter Nancy once stopped a parental argument with a Bible passage she had found and been saving just for such an occasion. "Never have grudges against others, or lose your temper, or raise your voice to anybody, or call each other names, or allow any sort of spitefulness" (Eph. 4:31 JB). Barbara said, "Phil and I just looked at her. Here we had a good fight going, and she stopped it with one Bible verse. I was so mad. Wasn't that stupid? I was angry because I no longer could *be* angry with a clear conscience."

Sometimes when we tell a friend exactly what we were fighting about with our children's other parent, it sounds so ridiculous we question our maturity. Katie was once discussing an intense fight she had with Tom over the fact that he had put the "wrong" pair of boots on Kurt to play in the snow. She went on and on, justifying her case on how irresponsible her ex-husband was, when Connie began to laugh. "You got to be kidding," Connie said, "at least he put *some* boots on Kurt. What's the big deal?"

What *was* the big deal? Again, it had nothing to do with the facts, it had to do with Katie's personal negative feelings over against her ex-husband. But in fighting with him, she hurt no one but herself and her children. Bitterness has no positive place in the relationship between ex-mates. It may make us feel "justified" temporarily, but it only destroys us in the end. One thing is sure: *our anger won't hurt our ex-mate; it will probably only foster anger on his or her part in return. But our anger* will *hurt our children.* Just as we once loved our ex-spouse very deeply, so our children now love us—*both* of us. They become confused and set adrift when the two people they love most of all indicate hatred towards each other. What possible good for our youngsters can come from our verbal avenging?

Proverbs gives some good advice in 15:1: "A soft answer turns away wrath, but a harsh word stirs up anger." There are times when we must bear the brunt of an ex-mate's anger in silence for the good of our children. It doesn't matter that the anger is unjustified; it doesn't matter that we are hurt deeply by it; what matters is the well-being of the children. Luther wrote:

> To suffer wrong destroys no one's soul, nay it improves the soul, even though it inflicts loss upon the body and property.

> But to do wrong—that destroys the soul even though it should gain all the world's wealth.

If we have the courage to analyze our faults and the real or supposed sins our ex-spouses have committed against us, we can have the courage to accept the forgiveness God has given us and to forgive transgressions against us in turn. Sometimes forgiveness is no easier to accept than it is to give. But both are possible with Christ's help. And once they are a reality in our lives, our lives change. The bad habits of nonforgiving transform into a good habit of forgiving. And once we forgive, we have little cause for bitterness or anger. We obtain peace, and in turn our children benefit. They have single parents who work together instead of against each other. And we single parents learn what love is really all about—perhaps for the first time in our lives. For "he who does not love does not know God; for God is love" (1 John 4:8).

GAMES PARENTS PLAY

Often, long after we've learned to control our anger for the most part, we continue to avenge ourselves in more subtle ways. We play games with the other parent partner—games in which our youngsters are the pawns. We battle back and forth on the chessboard of custody visitations, children's expenses, and who's the better parent. If we are checkmated, we simply set up the board once again and use a different offense and defense plan. But usually our game of chess is a stalemate. Nobody ever wins, and the children generally lose.

I SPY. The only thing I can remember about this game from childhood is that it began with one person saying, "I spy," and another responding, "What do you spy?" But that's not the way we play it with our children. We say to them, "I [want to] spy," and the youngster responds, "What do you [want to] spy?" A better translation of this game would be to admit, "I want to snoop, and I want you to tattle." Naturally we don't want our children to discuss our personal affairs with their other parent, but we see no problem in asking them to find out similar information for us. The youngsters may enjoy it for a while—it makes them feel important—but eventually they resent playing Benedict Arnold on either parent.

LET MERCURY DO IT. Mercury was the swift messenger of the Roman gods, and isn't it wonderful to have one or more of these messengers to serve us? Not that our ex-mates are gods, but it sure is great to let our children pass on information we'd rather not. If our youngsters ask, "When are you going to pay the back support check?" or inform, "Mom doesn't want us to stay overnight at your house next weekend," it saves us the unpleasant task of doing so. But it doesn't save our youngsters. The children hear one negative reaction when they carry the message from us, and they hear another negative when we receive the response. No wonder our children at one time or another tell us, "Find out yourself! I don't want to be your go-between anymore." Alas, we've lost the wing-footed god of messages. Mercury, however, was also the patron of thieves and gamblers, and we gamble with our children's wholesome parent–child relationship plus steal their rights to love both parents without interference when we "use" them to send our telegrams of unpleasant news.

TUG-OF-WAR. "Sometimes I feel like an old rag doll two little kids are fighting over," said 12-year-old Jennifer. My parents always fight over what I should do when. Daddy says I *must* come to his place; Mom says he's taking advantage of her generosity in visitation rights. Nobody ever asks me how I feel about it, or what I'd like to do. They just tug and tug, and I'm caught in the middle." Older children may have the courage and ability to speak out against Tug-Of-War, but younger ones are baffled by it and usually bear it in silent pain. We tug from one side; their other parent tugs from the other; and together we tear our little ones apart.

BUTTON, BUTTON, WHO'S GOT THE POISON BUTTON? This game should be labeled "Keep Out of Reach of Children!" Yet it is exactly to our children that we give our poison buttons —our verbal "putdowns" of their other parent. All our unvent bitterness regarding the details of our divorce or the failures of our ex-spouse are related in prejudicial statements such as:

I bet your father's apartment is a mess! He never picked up a thing when we were married.

Your mother may take you to church now, but I had to drag her out of bed every Sunday morning when you were little.

Well, I'm glad he bought *you* something. He was always too cheap to spend any money on me.

Oh, I'm a great cook! Your mom taught me how to put TV dinners in the oven the way she always did.

The scene from *Taking Sides,* by Norma Klein, in which a father slams the refrigerator door angrily and says, "If Phyllis has been filling your ears with a lot of garbage about. . . ." probably has a familiar ring to our youngsters. And they don't like it! None of us likes to hear ugly, snide remarks about people we love and respect. This version of Button, Button spews cyanide on ourselves and everyone it touches.

COURT-MARTIAL. "Your father got you home an hour late last Saturday, so he can't see you again for two weeks." "Your mother won't get another support check until she allows me my full privileges as father!" In cases as these, parents are court-martialed without a hearing. Yet the children are the ones to suffer the punishment.

LOOK WHAT HE (SHE) MADE ME DO! The object of this game is to blame the other parent for all one's personal failings. "That man makes me so upset, I forgot all about your school physical. Now we'll be lucky to get an appointment before class starts this fall." "If your mother wouldn't nag me all the time, I'd be more willing to cooperate. But she harps no matter what I do, so I might as well bend the visitation rules a bit to my advantage." This game is fun for parents because according to its rules, they are never responsible for their actions or inactions. It's impossible to set self-discipline as a goal for children, however, if the model they see is "justified" nondiscipline. Children pick up on this game quickly and soon use it against their siblings or parents. It's the oldest game in the world, and is recorded in Genesis 3:8-19.

SANTA CLAUS. We've already discussed this game—that of "buying" or assuring love via lavish gifts. Sometimes it's a coverup for the guilt a parent feels. It often ends up as a game of blackmail, however, for the more children receive, the more they expect. It's not a realistic family situation, and it puts hardships on everyone involved. The game begins in the happy-go-lucky "Flapper" era, but ends up in the Great Depression—an emotional depression for child and parent alike.

LET'S PRETEND. In Let's Pretend, the parent pretends the child is a substitute partner or friend. Going way beyond the limits of egalitarian living, the child is expected to fulfill a parent's need when they are lonely for friends or spouse. It may begin with the child hearing confidences regarding a parent's personal life, but it often ends with the child bearing burdens beyond its years. "I hate it when Dad tells me all about his dates," said one teenage boy. "He pretends we're equals—both teenagers—and thinks we should discuss our girlfriends. It's so childish of him. I hate it!" Another son said, "My mother expects me to solve all her problems now that Dad's gone. I have enough of my own, and I don't know what to do about hers anyway. But I feel guilty because she *thinks* I can help and expects me to."

GAMES CHILDREN PLAY

Children play games too. They play their parents off against each other for their own benefit within two-parent families, but only in single-parent families are they likely to get away with it consistently. Purposely or not purposely, they take advantage of their new situation with one or another of the following games.

KEEP AWAY. Keeping Mom away from Dad and vice versa is the best game children can play. They can reap all kinds of rewards if their parents don't communicate, for then they can tell each parent whatever they want without fear of discovery. Sometimes children claim a parent neglects them to arouse sympathy from the other parent and get additional benefits. Or they say a parent definitely said "No" to a request when the parent really said "Maybe." A call between the parents would bring out the truth, but when parents are bitter and noncommunicating, the child's game is easy to win.

POOR LITTLE MATCH GIRL. This game is easy to play with parents who feel guilty or are afraid of losing their child's love. "Mom, I think I'll stay with Dad this weekend because you never take me anywhere anyway. It's such a drag now that there's never any money for fun. I've been dying to go horseback riding, and maybe Dad can scrape up the money to take me." Many a mother, low-income or not, will respond to the call of her poor little "baby's" needs. She's been blackmailed and responds with bribery. The Poor Little Match Girl game often depends upon Keep Away. "Mom always lets me stay out until . . ." or "Daddy understands how I feel so he . . . ." Another variation relates to the "I didn't ask to be born" routine many a child from two-parent families uses to try to extort privileges. In our case, it's, "Poor me. Because of your divorce, I'm the loser" with the implication, "Don't you think you ought to make it up to me by . . . ?"

MAN THE TORPEDOES. This game is the child's version of Court-Martial. The child does everything he can to torpedo his parents. Any misbehavior that hurts father or mother will do, from simple disobedience of family rules to getting into serious trouble with the law. The child is angry and wants to punish his parents for the divorce, or for what he feels is lack of attention, or for any real or imagined wrong. When this is carried to extremes, professional help may be needed.

CHILDREN'S NEED FOR ADULT MODELS

Sometimes, because of the games single parents play against each other and because of the games children play on both, the custodial parent feels it would be better all around if the less the child sees of the noncustodial parent, the better. This is almost always not true, however. *Boys and girls need men and women adult models from which to learn what it means to be a man or a woman.* A boy growing up in a household of women suffers from his lack of contact with adult males. "I've been miserable ever since we came to live with Grandma," one 13-year-old said. "I wanted to go out for football, and Grandma said it was too rough. Mom wouldn't let me go skiing with my friends because she said it was too dangerous. They understand my sisters, but they don't understand what it's like to be a boy. Sometimes I think they'd turn me into a girl if they could. They keep saying my sisters don't give them the trouble I do."

Girls living with their father also miss a female adult's influence. "I love being with Daddy, but there're just some things about being a girl my mom understands more." Neither sex is by nature more equipped than the other to meet all the needs of children as they grow up. God's plan was to give children both mother and father, and if life has changed the plan, then it is all the more important for the two single parents to be conscious of their children's need for the other adult.

Sometimes a substitute "parent" can fulfill this role if the real one lives far away or does not take the responsibility seriously. We've all experienced cases in which our children found someone else's mother or father easier to talk to than us. It hurts a bit, and perhaps we can't understand it at the time, but then one day we hear our children mention that such-and-such a friend thinks we're more "with it" than the child's own parents. We've had other adult models in our childhood years that spoke to our distinct interests and needs besides our parents—an uncle, for example, or a gym teacher, or the single lady living down the street. If these people filled a positive influence in our lives, why should we have a problem with other adults helping us meet the needs of our offspring?

REMARRIAGE OF EX-MATE

When our ex-mate remarries, a third person enters the lives of our children, and readjustments must be made. Just as it's difficult to understand the feelings and reactions of our youngsters' other parent, so it is even more difficult to understand those of his or her new spouse. *But they are in the most difficult position of all.* They are outsiders, new to the family—and ours *is* a family even if we are separated. They married a man or woman, and his or her children came along with the deal. They may resent the children or the family income delegated to "child support." The children may loom as a threat to their security, for allegiances to one's children run strong. These new spouses are never more than "stepmothers" or "stepfathers," at least in the beginning, and the very terms ring with negative connotations.

Ex-mates also have compounded problems regarding relationships to their children. They married in response to their needs and feelings—when they and their new spouses were ready. But their children may *not* be ready. *"He* gets the attention *I* used to get," complained one ten-year-old. "Mom used to take *me* to the movies; now she goes with *him*," complained another. Children are often jealous and resentful of their parent's new spouse. They feel they see little enough of their other parent without having to share that precious time with a "rival."

When my daughter was ten I was dating a man whom she liked very much. But when Jan thought I might marry him, she said, "You won't marry *anyone* for at least 15 years, will you?" At 25 she felt she would be safely beyond adapting to a new father. But just as your ex-spouse faced these problems, you may also. Statistics indicate that 80% of people remarry after a first divorce; five out of six men, and three out of four women. Unless you are one of the 20% who remain single, you will need some serious planning and adapting to do, and one way is to begin now to understand those same adjustments your former mate and new spouse are undertaking. Helping them help your children to adjust may help *you* sooner than you think.

Don't expect your children's first negative reactions to a new parent to continue indefinitely. They may be uncomfortable with this person for a while. They may not like the changes they feel the person has made in their relationship with their other parent, but there'll probably be something about the person they'll like very much. And if the step-parent is patient and loving, your youngsters will react in the same measure. They may even begin to feel disloyal to you because they have unexpected feelings of love for your "substitute." It is important to reassure them that *true love, like God's, is boundless.* It is not limited to one, two, or a few people. It is not like a cake that can be cut in just so many pieces. It runs like a spring that never dries up.

Similarly, do not let yourself become jealous over your ex-mate's new-found happiness. You have no idea what joy our Lord may have in store for you. Besides, what you had with him or her can never be taken away. Marriage is so close a relationship that time can never erase its memories completely. Decades in the future the "negatives" may be largely forgotten, and the "positives" remain. *Many ex-spouses become better friends over the years.* Even now, your former husband or wife may think far more highly of you than his or her actions and words indicate. Going through a divorce is like walking through a fire. One gets burned— physically, mentally, emotionally. All one experiences at first is pain. And then for years the scars remain. A person who feels pain—a person who sees evidence of the scars daily—is likely to lash out against the hurt. But as God heals our lives, he also changes our attitudes and memories.

LOVE'S HEALING

It is never too early to begin this healing process. In discussing problems with your children's other parent, remember these words:

A word fitly spoken
  is like apples of gold in a setting of silver.
Like a gold ring or an ornament of gold
  is a wise reprover to a listening ear (Prov. 25:11-12).

It is important that you are honest with your ex-spouse, but also loving. Include these attributes in your action plan when dealing with any factors regarding your children.

You must speak the truth to one another, since we are all parts of one another. Even if you are angry, you must not sin: never let the sun set on your anger or else you will give the devil a foothold (Eph. 3:25-26 JB).

Divorce is no excuse for a lack of Christian love between ex-partners. No matter what one or the other has done in the past, Christ calls us to forgive. Remember that Bible passage Barbara's daughter read to stop her parents' argument? "Never have grudges against others, or lose your temper, or raise your voices to anybody, or call each other names, or allow any sort of spitefulness." It ends with words most apropos to single parents:

Be friends with one another, and kind, forgiving each other as readily as God forgave you in Christ (Eph. 4:31-32 JB).

"Whatever happened to that love we had? Whatever happened to that inexplicable joy we shared together?" *It can still be there.* No, not as man and wife, but as father and mother. The joy of watching our children grow up and mature, with each of us contributing our utmost to their benefit, can be a unique inexplicable joy we share.

If "of all sad words of tongue or pen the saddest are these: 'It might have been!' " then why let it happen to you? Why not follow John's advice: "Let us love one another; for love is of God, and he who loves is born of God and knows God" (1 John 4:7)? If there is any possible way to build a good relationship with our children's other parent, why neglect it? Our children can only benefit, and so will we! It'll make future dealings with that parent pleasant instead of unpleasant. It'll be a major step to that "abundant life" Christ has promised us. It'll help us understand what the "God [who] is love" is all about.

"Love one another as I have loved you" (John 13:34).

8

A New Beginning—
A New You

"I think I'm going through an identity crisis," my 14-year-old said on the way to church this morning. "I look at my face in a mirror, and I wonder who that person is. I talk, and my voice doesn't sound like it should belong to my face. I think it's strange that my friends look at this face and hear this voice and think it's me. I don't. I'm trying to find out who *is* me."

WHO ARE YOU?

"Mirror, mirror on the wall. Who is the fairest of them all?" singsonged the queen in Snow White day after day. She thought she knew who she was. Then one day the mirror didn't respond positively, and suddenly the queen also had an identity crisis. Hers turned her into a witch.

Most of us know who we are, we think. Actually, we don't give much thought to it. We're Ann, or Joe, or Betty, whoever. That's who we are. What more is there? And then one day the mirror of our lives cracks, and we are totally lost. We suddenly have no identities. "Who are you?" I wrote myself 18 years ago. "I thought I knew you. But now who are you, anyway?"

Who are *you?* Do you know really? If someone were to ask you to tell who you are in a sentence or two, could you respond? Who is this person that has been you all these years? What makes him or her tick?

Try doing what my daughter did. Take a look at yourself in a mirror. Look at your face. Ignore any aging signs; everyone is aging. Look at *you.* Especially look at your eyes. Do your eyes tell you anything about yourself?

What do you see in the mirror? Sadness? Tiredness? Determination? Mischievousness? Get a pad and pencil and write down what you see. Think about something that happened in the past and watch your eyes. Now try the present. The future. How do your eyes react when your children flash across your mind? What about your ex-mate? Marriage? Career? God? Jot down the thoughts and your eyes' reactions. Put away the pad when you become bored. But save it.

During the next few weeks, make a logbook of "extreme" reactions to everyday life. If you're depressed because of something that happens at home or work, write it down. Then record the time of day and what happened just before you felt "down." Record both positive and negative extreme reactions. Don't worry if one outweighs the other. This is no test. This is just a written photograph of how you react at present. After a month or so, read your logbook. You'll be surprised to see a pattern of activities, conditions, people who make you feel positive or negative. You can use this information in restyling your life towards the positive.

This chapter is dedicated to you. It's dedicated to your own personal situation analysis. This cannot be done in a day or week—perhaps not in years—but any analysis of what you are and what you really want in life will be a first step to making an action plan for your personal future. Right now you may be chasing the wrong rainbows. You may be following set patterns which you think you want, but which really were given to you by others along the way. You may be running down a yellow brick road that never leads to Emerald City. Or perhaps the emeralds you are seeking aren't emeralds at all—just mirages.

WHERE ARE YOU?

Where are you right now? Still wrapped up in grief? Still unable to forget the past and begin a new life? C. S. Lewis wrote after the death of his wife that part of his misery was the fact that he didn't merely suffer, but he kept thinking about the fact he suffered. "I not only live each endless day in grief, but live each day thinking about living each day in grief."

Of course, one can't deny or hurry grief. Grief is a natural reaction to a loss. We wouldn't be human if we didn't react to death or divorce with grief, and sometimes even depression. Our Lord was extremely depressed as the result of grief. He said to his disciples in the Garden of Gethsemane, "My soul is very sorrowful, even to death" (Mark 14:34).

Katie understood depression. She had been taught to accept God's will, but she wanted to scream at him or at fate for the pain she felt. Her minister preached sermon after sermon on "Praising the Lord no matter what," and Katie only sank deeper and deeper into grief. She felt guilty over her natural reactions to pain and the changes in her life.

Katie's guilt was unwarranted, however. There is "a time to weep, and a time to laugh; a time to mourn, and a time to dance" (Eccl. 3:4). No one would walk up to Christ in Gethsemane as "his sweat became like great drops of blood" and push away the "angel from heaven strengthening him" (Luke 22:43-44) to say, "Hey, stop that sorrowing! Praise the Lord! Just praise the Lord!" No, *only after one has experienced the depths of grief can one truly reach the heights of praise.* It's healthy to take the time to work out grief. "Wait for the Lord, be strong, and let your heart take courage" (Ps. 27:14). After grief comes praise.

> I waited patiently for the Lord; he inclined to me
>> and heard my cry.
> He drew me up from the desolate pit, out of the miry bog,
>> and set my feet upon a rock, making my steps secure.
> He put a new song in my mouth,
>> a song of praise to our God (Ps. 40:1-3).

Perhaps it is a different reaction you are now experiencing. Maybe you feel exactly as our children do over the loss of a parent. You can't stop wondering, "What's going to happen to me?" None of your worries or fears can compare to those of the widow recorded in 2 Kings 4, however. Her husband had served in the ministry of the great prophet Elisha. As a faithful servant of the Lord, he had concentrated on his service rather than on building up financial security for his retirement. When he died, he left such enormous debts that his wife turned to Elisha in great anxiety and fear because she had no means to pay them, and "the creditor has come to take my two children to be slaves."

Do you know anyone with such debts? Anyone with so great a fear? It's even difficult for us to imagine. Thank God we don't live in an age where our debts are forcibly redeemed by the sale of our most precious gifts into slavery.

"It's a hard-knock life," sing the little girls in the New York orphanage in the musical *Annie*. There is nothing you or I have gone through that someone else didn't before we. There is no tale of horror we can relate that someone can't match or better. That doesn't make it any easier on us, of course. Usually we're so wrapped up in our problems we can't even relate to those of others, let alone sympathize.

St. Paul speaks of the "thorn in his flesh" in 2 Corinthians 12:7 and of the three times he asked the Lord to remove it. But Paul

116

says God's answer was, "My grace is sufficient for you, for my power is made perfect in weakness." *Weakness. The only way God's power is perfected is in weakness.* In *A Grief Observed,* C. S. Lewis says, "He always knew that my temple was a house of cards. His only way of making me realize the fact was to knock it down."

People who have gone through pain and recovered successfully have learned to overlook the hurts of the past. *That's what forgiveness is all about: letting go of the past!* When we do that we can also overlook the imperfections of the present. We can dwell on the positives instead. Ten years ago my mother-in-law and I were looking at the scene outside the living room picture window. She commented on its beauty—the field across the road and the suggestion of the lake that lay behind some trees. "Yes, but look over there," I said, pointing to the service station at the left of the field. "Look at all those old junk cars rusting in the lot." I couldn't believe she thought the scene was lovely. Every time I looked out, those cars spoiled my view. "Oh, learn to look *over* them," she advised. "Don't let that ugliness spoil the beauty."

My mother also believes in forgetting the hurts of the past. She feels the past *is* past. "It's over and done with; why dwell on it?" she's remarked, referring to disappointments in her younger years. As a result, her outlook on life is a healthy one. She lives in the present and in the future. Both are a positive vitality in her thoughts and actions.

Fear. Anxiety. Depression. In a recent article on depression from a popular family magazine, the author says that *a sign of depression is when we decide unconsciously that it's safer to feel miserable and exhausted all the time than to change our lives.* This kind of depression should be a warning to us that "we are neglecting something very important: ourselves." Her words reminded me of verse I wrote when I was in the indecisive, "I don't want to change" frame of mind years ago.

some people
never make up their minds.
they never say
i will or
i won't,
wanting neither this
nor that,
just some of
both,
without either . . .

some people
never make up their minds
to live.
insecure cowards,
they want reality
in unreality,
walking down
the up escalator,
for using escalators
saves energy . . .

Inertia is the "tendency to stay in motion when in motion and to remain at rest when at rest." Or at least that's how I remember it from grade school science. If you and I are "at rest," we aren't going to make any changes in our lives. We aren't going to find out who we are. We aren't going to be open to God's rich gifts filling us to the brim. We're just going to stagnate. We're just going to gather moss. We're just going to continue in our misery.

LOVING AND ACCEPTING YOURSELF

Try for a moment to picture a door that has all your problems painted on it. Now imagine yourself walking through it and letting God close the door behind you. How do you feel?

Now take out that mirror again. Look at yourself. Say, "I totally love and accept you as you are." Could you say that? Or did you stumble over the words?

It's difficult for most of us to let God close the door behind us on our problems. But it is more possible to do that than to say that we "love and accept" ourselves. Perhaps the former is easier because we remember trusting in God completely as young children. Our evening prayer was based on Psalm 4:8:

In peace I will both lie down and sleep;
For thou alone, O Lord, makest me dwell in safety.

Ah, but loving and accepting ourselves, that's a different story. Yet *"I totally love you and accept you as you are" is what God says to us every day of our lives.* He's not talking about our sins; he's forgiven them. He's not talking about our righteous acts; he says they are as impressive as menstrual cloths, or "filthy rags," as the King James version tactfully translates the Hebrew. God's talking about us! Us as individuals. Each one of us. His own creation. He loves and accepts us! Not for *what* we are, but *because* we are.

God expects us to love and accept ourselves too. He commands, "Love your neighbor as *yourself.*" I don't know if you love yourself. I know there was a time I didn't love myself. As a matter of fact, I didn't think I should. It seemed selfish. Then I read Eric Fromm's *The Art of Loving,* and I changed my mind. One quote intrigued me: "Immature love says 'I love you because I need you,' and mature love says 'I need you because I love you.' " The latter seemed like a good definition of healthy love.

Fromm says that selfishness and self-love are not identical, but opposites. Selfish people are incapable of loving others, but they are also incapable of loving themselves. On the other hand, if an individual is able to love productively, he loves himself too; if he can love only others, he cannot love at all.

Perhaps that was the message Luther intended when he advised his associate Philip Melanchthon to "Sin boldly, but believe yet more boldly." Melanchthon was a scholarly, quiet individual, quite different in personality from Luther. To this cautious cleric, Luther says in effect, "Live! Don't be so afraid of sinning. Trust in the grace of God. *Live, and when you sin, depend on his mercy."*

So let's begin. Let's discard the past, and live the present. Let's learn who we are and accept it. Let's change what we don't like and build on what we do!

Connie said the first thing she had to do to make a new start was to stop feeling a failure. When her marriage ended, she felt she had failed as a wife. With no other measure by which to judge herself, she could only proclaim, "Guilty!" It is true that in the past, society has largely measured a married woman's success by how well she pleased her husband and how good a mother she was. A man's worth was not judged first as a spouse and father, however. If his marriage ended, he still had an identity in his work. But even women who worked full time were led to believe they had the main responsibility of keeping a marriage and family together, or at least the major blame if it fell apart.

But the times, "they are a-changing." Both men and women, husbands and wives, fathers and mothers, share God's command of love—marital and parental. Paul says "there is no male or female, for you are all one in Christ Jesus" (Gal. 3:28). We are all identical in God's eyes. Man or woman, each of us has an identity of our own. If forgiveness is letting go of the past, then it's time for us to forgive ourselves and our past sins, just as our Lord has. It's time to discard our negative images of ourselves and look forward instead to a new life, renewed in Christ Jesus.

YOUR CHANGING ROLE

One way women can do this is to tackle a realistic fact of life—working. Perhaps we didn't have a full-time job in the past, but we probably do now. And more than likely it brings us new problems in raising our children. We simply don't have enough time and energy to keep up with both work responsibility and our children's needs. We feel guilty because we must divide our time between them.

Realistically, however, we never did devote 100% of our time to our children. We filled our days with church and school and personal activities that often conflicted with our children's schedules. When your children came home from school, did you stop your housework or cooking or laundry to spend a few hours with them? Did they even expect that? Or would they have liked that day after day?

Now we're not there when our youngsters come home. However, now we're more likely to make a point of setting time aside in the evening to devote to their interests and problems. We felt we were always there before. It didn't occur to us then that we weren't "always there" to our children any more than our mates were "always there" to us even when they were in the same room. And the activities of our former lives that we've sacrificed to work full-time probably are the daytime "extras" we engaged in, not necessarily those that dealt with the children. The trade-off may not be nearly as great as it appears without closer examination.

WORKING AND MOTHERING

In *Your Child Is a Person,* psychiatrists Chess, Thomas, and Birch say that "the fact that good mothering is important does not mean that it has to be administered twenty-four hours a day every day. The question is whether a good mother who works can still give her child adequate nurturing and love in the hours she spends at home with him." The doctors go on to say that if a mother and child don't get along, they'll keep on disagreeing unless there's a correction in attitude; merely stopping work "won't mend things." In fact, sometimes a mother's working "improves her relationship with her children." The adult stimulation at work may result in "a resurgence of motherly love" upon the parent's arrival home, and her children will "share the benefits of [her] greater relaxation and cheerfulness."

A recent issue of my daughter's *Teen* magazine reported the results of a poll of teenagers with working mothers. Many of the teenagers polled reported that their working mothers were "happier, less bored, more independent, and had more to talk about because of outside interests." Many, also, liked their newfound privacy, and felt the latter gave them time to be alone and apart, "something we really need." I guess that is what my daughter meant when she responded to my staying home for a week's vacation last month. By Thursday Jan said, "I hope you don't take this wrong, but I don't like your being home all the time. When I get home from school, I like to have some time to myself—to listen to records, to read, to 'bum around'—without a mother being around to be a 'parent.' "

"Working Mothers: What Science Really Knows," a Fall 1980 article in the *Chicago Tribune,* states that one out of every two school-age children in this country has a mother who works outside the home, and that by 1990, 10.5 million children under the age of six will have working mothers. Referring to a report by the American Academy of Pediatrics on whether mothers' working did their infants harm, the article reported that researchers found it difficult to test infants, toddlers, and preschoolers. However much of what they did find about children who grew up with working mothers was positive. These children had "higher aspirations, broader concepts of sex roles, better peer orientation, and more independence and responsibility."

It is, of course, over our infants and preschoolers where we suffer the most guilt. Yet probably we have no choice but to work at least part-time. In such cases, our substitute becomes all the more important. A father can care for and "mother" an infant with the same nurturing effect a mother can. This is true, also, of another adult if the person is loving and sincere in taking on this responsibility. The psychiatrists mentioned earlier studied cases in which young children were separated from their mothers and given good substitute care. Of particular note were children who were evacuated from their families during the blitz of London and placed in nurseries away from the city for one to five years. Their mothers visited them whenever possible. When these children were examined as young adults, the study could find "no evidence that separation from the mother as such had any serious effects in the development of the group studied."

Yet finding good substitute child care is one of single parents' biggest problems. And when we are fortunate enough to find a real gem, we often cannot afford the price. In 1980, 90% of all working women earned less than $15,000, yet most single female parents had custody of their children. It is difficult enough to find good substitute care for young children, but when it depends upon paying a price most women cannot afford, it becomes necessary to find another solution. It goes without saying that if you are fortunate enough to have a relative or friend who will care for your children while you work, your problems have greatly diminished. Sometimes a church congregation includes a person who can help. Licensed homes, day-care centers, or nursery schools are other solutions, though generally less satisfactory. There usually is no easy answer. There never has been. Surely this is a time to place trust in our Lord's words, "Ask, and it will be given to you" (Matt. 7:7).

YOUR CAREER PROBLEMS

In 1970 a research associate in The Office of Education's National Center for Educational Research and Development predicted that within a decade sexual discrimination in job opportunities would disappear or at least be mitigated, and corporations would provide day-care centers for children of working mothers.

It's no doubt safe to say there's no day-care center at your place of work. This prediction is far from a reality. Nor has "sexual discrimination in job opportunities disappeared." In fact, in some professions sexual ratios have reversed. In 1879, for example, women comprised more than 33% of faculty positions in U. S. colleges and universities; in 1970 the ratio was less than 25%, with not even 1% holding department chairs. A century ago 80%

of elementary school principals were women; in 1970 80% were men. A current study by the management-consulting firm of Heidrick & Struggles places only 6% of working women in management or administrative roles.

It was in 1963 that federal legislation guaranteed women "equal pay for equal work." Yet today women need a college degree to earn more than a man does with an eighth-grade education. *U.S. News and World Report* reported in January, 1979, "At the latest count, male high school dropouts earned, on the average, $1,604 more a year than women college graduates."

In 1955, the average working woman earned $63.90 for the average man's $100; in 1960 she earned $60.80; in 1970 she earned only $58.10; and in 1981, her pay ratio was no better than twenty years previously. Currently women fill almost 50% of *all* jobs, but they fill over 75% of the secretarial and clerical positions. When a job is something only women do, it is valued less. Salaries go up when men do certain jobs, as shown in the pay for paramedics; salaries go down when women do certain jobs, such as when women became bank tellers, a position once exclusively male.

Because of these realities, now's the time to make a situation analysis of all the job opportunities open to women. You may need some night courses in secretarial work, keypunching, and the like, but *it's wise to begin thinking of your work as a career instead of a job* so that you raise your sights to a future goal— one more beneficial to you both personally and financially. A letter to the Women's Bureau, U.S. Department of Labor, 200 Constitution Avenue, N. W. Washington, D. C. 20210 asking for information regarding job opportunities should prove helpful. You've probably considered retail-store clerking, waitressing, secretarial work, and other typical "female" work roles, but also look at the random list below and see if any of these work activities open to women interest you:

bus/cab driver	tailoring
bank guard	hairdressing
electrician	home typing
mechanic	keypunch operator
bank teller	school hot-lunch cook
real estate agent	nursery-school aide
mail carrier	nurses aide
landscaping	domestic service
telephone operator	companion/housekeeper
retail-sales manager	baby-sitting service
customer-service rep	licensed home for pre-
tutoring	schoolers

YOUR CAREER REWARDS

Changing your attitude about working and finding a position that is satisfying and challenging will also change *you.* A 1977 nationwide survey reported in the *Journal of Marketing* regarding the modern feminine life-style divided full-time home-makers and full-time working women into either "traditional" or "modern" camps. (As reported earlier, only 13% of all American women today are in the "traditional" full-time homemaker category.) The study proved that a "nontraditional feminine orienta-tion does not mean an unfeminine person." On the contrary, working women "took more interest in their personal appearance and looking attractive" than did their counterparts. They were "more concerned for physical conditioning, more cosmopolitan and liberal in their interests and attitudes, more pragmatic about financial matters [and] more tolerant of views dissimilar to theirs."

In a nutshell, *most working women look and feel better about themselves than women who have no paying jobs outside the home.* They become proud of their accomplishments because they are *acknowledged* as accomplishments. It is unfair that full-time

125

housewives too often receive no similar acknowledgement, for they surely deserve it. Unfortunately this is because our society still relates personal worth to financial success or independence, a misguided value judgment. Thus former housewives who are forced suddenly to find employment may just as suddenly become proud that they receive financial reward for the work they do. Sometimes receiving a first paycheck changes their images of themselves. As Barbara said recently, "It's beautiful how women who are forced to enter the work market blossom into people in their own right after a few years. They are scared to death at first, but after plunging into the cold water, they adjust and finally swim lengths they never did before."

Connie remarked how working improved her social life as a single person, particularly her dating life. "I keep running into men over 35 who had traditional wives at their own request, but now are attracted to me as a working woman. Many of them say they made a mistake in not allowing their wives to "grow" along with them. Their wives had fine minds, but never leaving the home limited their over-all growth." Jack told me his ex-wife became complacent and lazy. She lost interest in her personal appearance. "I'll never ask a woman not to work again; in fact I'll insist she work at least part-time to keep her active and vital. I want a wife I can talk to."

Toni Tucci, a 60-year-old author who looks a glamorous 40, agrees. In *Mileage* she says that women who never "grow old" are women who remain active, exercise curiosity every day, and never allow themselves to get bored. "You should never waste the precious lifetime that God has given you," she writes. Rather "all your energy should be directed to making your life a full one, rather than preventing it from changing." The author remarks that everywhere one turns these days, there are women going off into new directions which would have terrified them twenty years ago. Such women are giving themselves new lives.

YOUR CHANGING SOCIAL LIFE

It takes about two years for most of us to bridge the worlds between married and divorced/widowed. During those two years of constant struggle, it seems like everything we had has been taken away. But from the beginning we've begun to use personal talents we may not have known existed. We've tapped strength that may never have needed such tapping before. We've learned to lean on God in place of a mate, and by God's help we've learned to lean on ourselves. We've looked at our parenthood with opened eyes, and consciously or subconsciously taught our children to be more self-reliant. We've learned so much, sometimes through trial and error, but we'll never be the same again. We'll never be as helpless in any sense as we were before. We have already put to use more talents that lay hidden previously.

Yet often we're lonely. The longer we were married, the lonelier we may feel. The worlds of the married and the formerly married are universes apart. We never noticed the subculture of singles when we were married. It existed right under our noses, yet we had no idea of its existence, let alone any conception of what it was all about.

Now we do. Now it's as though we've taken blinders off and put on wide-ranged glasses. Now we see *all* adults and we identify with them all. Barbara was surprised how quickly she built up a new network of friends among single people. "I realize how few friends—married friends—Phil and I had together," she said. "Most of our married friends were really only 'acquaintances.' We socialized together, but we weren't true friends, true intimates. I liked one or another of the couple better than Phil did. And vice versa. But now I have some really close friends."

In his book *Friendship,* Joel D. Block says the odds are against married people "finding a compatible foursome. Each person has to like two people, for a total of eight likes." He also states that only 6% of married people have an opposite-sex friend, and even

127

same-sex friendships among the married are hardly abundant. In comparison, *single men and women "are more than twice as likely as their married counterparts to have close friends."*

"Maybe," we react doubtfully. No matter what Barbara or this author says, many of us feel we had many more friends before we became single again. *All types of organizations have been formed to meet the needs of singles.* One of the first was *Parents Without Partners.* It has chapters throughout the country which can be identified through its international office at 7910 Wood-month Ave., Washington D.C. 20014. The *National Association of Christian Singles* central office is P.O. Box 11394, Kansas City MO 64112. Minneapolis and other large cities host Christian Singles Conferences for all ages sponsored annually by *Lutheran Young Adult/Singles Ministry, Inc.,* 1101 University Ave. S.E., Minneapolis MN 55414. In Chicago C.L.A.S. *(Chicagoland Association of Singles)* lists over thirty different singles groups in its newsletter, many of which are church-affiliated. Check locally to see what single groups are available to you.

Few of us are fortunate enough to have single-adult friends when we reenter the single life. Many of our friends are married, and some think it's out of place for us to attend single parties, dances, events to meet new people. They believe the stereotypes that such places are dens of iniquity. Pastor Nicholas Christoff, the nationally known "Singles Pastor" of the American Lutheran Church disagrees. "You know, singles are not as reckless as society is led to believe. Nothing is worse or more damaging than to be hurt in a relationship. Singles have seen that and have grown from that. You have to hear their hurt and reaffirm them in their purpose."

Connie said she got so tired of her mother asking her, "What will people think?" if she joined a singles group. Barbara laughed and said that question reminded her of some lines in Robert Burns' "To a Louse":

Oh wad some power the giftie gie us
to see oursels as others see us!

The little louse crawling on the fine hat of the proper lady attending church went completely unnoticed by the hat's owner. She would have been appalled had she realized a louse was ruining her proud image. Pride and ignorance of what one goes through upon first reentering single life should not curtail our efforts to find new friendships. *What counts is not what people think. What counts is what God thinks.* And God does not want us to be lonely. He loves us, and he knows constant loneliness is not good for us or for our children. He wants us to find friends who add joy to our lives.

In addition to meeting new friends at single social functions, we can find meaningful relationships by attending classes. Taking a class that meets once a week for six to twelve weeks gives one something to look forward to. It also gives us the opportunity to learn to know others gradually and to see which ones share common values and interests. It gives us the chance to melt the ice instead of having to break it at a one-time event.

Right after high school a friend of mine began taking a class in stereophonic equipment. She met her future husband there. When he died some years later, Bonnie went on to university night classes both to get a better job and also to meet stimulating people. I took dance lessons when my marriage ended years ago and also a chess class at the local YMCA. Both classes added new dimensions and interests in my life. Barbara took auto mechanics (she's the practical one in the group), and Connie took French. Katie said those classes were too easy; she was going to make up one of her own—one that was the most difficult class a woman could take. She titled it "Eating Out Alone." Another version is "Going to a Movie Alone." Such "classes" in becoming a friend to oneself are as important to a single person's growth as the ones in which other goals are pursued.

YOUR NEW LOVE

Most people view their single life as temporary, and their main goal in socializing is to find a new spouse. Sometimes they are so insecure or unhappy being single that they make wrong decisions about a future mate. They marry someone exactly like their first spouse—a tendency that brings problems. Obviously if you and one type of person had difficulty making a past marriage work, why would you both have any less difficulty the second time around?

It's often difficult to analyze a person we think we love or to analyze our relationship. We project onto that person what we think we see—what we'd like to see. We're so in love and happy that we're not alone anymore, that we're blind to any difficulties that could arise in the future. In Dorothy Tennov's *Love and Limerence, The Experience of Being in Love,* the author points up the pitfalls of romantic love. The problem is the characteristics of something she coins "limerence"—the initial feeling of being in love. During limerence, the emotions take over and rational thinking is pushed back. The loved one is without imperfection. No matter what our age, and no matter how many times it happens, when we first "fall in love," we are so overcome with joyful emotion that we see, feel, know, only that love.

This emotional state can last up to two years before any reality sets in. If the relationship goes beyond that, it's a good chance that we've passed the initial "in love" stage and have reached a deeper state of "loving." But often along the way we begin to have doubts. We push them back into our subconscious because we want so desperately to love, and to be loved. Yet when doubts crop up, it's a good idea to write them down for future analysis. I usually write some verse about what I'm feeling. If that's not your style, just doodle. Everyone can do that. Relax. Then draw and write whatever comes to mind. Don't think about it. Don't force it. Just jot down pictures, notes, comments, and feelings as they occur.

130

Perhaps you'll write a catch phrase over and over that later will give you a clue as to what's bothering you.

I was once having a disagreement with a man I had considered marrying. He was very upset and angry. As he lectured on and on, I simply doodled on a grocery bag, and commented now and then verbally. It was calming to write rather than to respond in anger. After a while I realized I had written my name and was tracing it over and over. The more he demanded I change to meet his female role expectations, the larger my name became. It was a little thing, perhaps, but seeing it later made me realize any permanent relationship with this man would never be "permanent." We were too different. If we ever married, I couldn't be me and he couldn't be he. It wasn't a question of who was right or wrong. It wasn't a question of feeling for each other. It just wouldn't work.

People tend to grasp relationships or to stay in wrong ones for them because they decide any is better than none. "I'll keep him until something better comes along," Connie once said. "Why?" we asked. "You're so miserable." It's true that no other person is ever going to meet one's total expectations or needs, and compromise is always a fact of life, but to settle for little compatability is wasteful. *One is not a failure to break off a relationship or friendship that is filled with more negatives than positives; one is more of a failure if one can't.* "Why wait until something better comes along?" Barbara asked Connie. "Nothing better is likely as long as you're not free to be open to it."

No one's worth is dependent on their marital status. However, whether we wish to marry soon, later, or never, most of us do enjoy the company of the opposite sex. And once again we meet the judgment of family and friends. "Where did you meet him?" they ask. In their minds, there are "proper" and "improper" places to meet the opposite sex. And they have endless taboos, opinions, and convictions regarding two people's relationship while single.

Again, it is only God's opinion that matters. Only God understands you, and this person, and the circumstances that brought you together. A long time ago—way back in my confirmation class—my pastor pointed to a picture of Christ and told us to let Christ's presence be the guide in anything we did in our lives. If Christ could appear physically in the midst of any of our activities and we would feel comfortable with him there, then we would have his approval. So then, let your actions be between you and your Lord. If you mistakenly "sin boldly" in a non-God-pleasing way, then pick yourself up and "believe yet more boldly." God will forgive your sins and errors in judgment. Ask as did David after sinning, "Create in me a clean heart, O God, and renew a right spirit within me" (Ps. 51:10).

GOD'S GIFTS TO YOU

Remember the parable of the talents (Matt. 25:14-29)? In this parable a man entrusts his servants with money, units of about $1000 called "talents." The servants who received five and two talents each "traded" (invested) them and doubled their value. But the servant who received one talent "went and dug in the ground and hid his master's money." Imagine, for a minute, if you gave $8000 to three different investors. You'd be very happy with the $5000 and $2000 investments which doubled, but disappointed and displeased with the investor who took your $1000 and did nothing with it. So was the master. "You wicked and slothful servant! . . . You ought to have invested my money with the bankers, and at my coming I should have received what was my own with interest."

It is ironical that Christians can listen to this parable read in church year after year and nod, agreeing, yet never apply it to their own unique talents. *It is ironical that men and women who teach their children not to be wasteful do exactly that with portions of their own lives.*

God has given each of us far more than one talent. We've received many gifts to develop and expand to God's use and our fulfillment. But too often we hide our talent, waiting for everything to be "perfect" in life before we bring it out and use it. God says that is "wicked and slothful," and in truth we fail to use our talents because we are selfish and lazy. It's easier to just keep living each day the same way year after year. It's too much trouble to find out who we are and what talents we've received. It's easier to say everyone else has the talents; poor us, we've none. It's easy to procrastinate, saying we'll use our talents to the fullest when we find the perfect mate, the perfect job, the perfect life as we see it. It's easy to "play God" with God's gifts.

We've all heard the expression "Include me out." When it comes to your single life, ask God to "Exclude me in." St. Mark writes "Therefore I tell you, whatever you ask in prayer, believe that you receive it, and you will" (Mark 11:24). God can "exclude" you "in" his love from the isolation, rejection, loneliness, and feelings of unworthiness that are common to the newly single. "For God is at work in you, both to will and to work for his good pleasure" (Phil. 2:13). He can exclude you from the bad, and include you in the good at any stage in your life.

God can make you a person in your own right. He can give you knowledge and understanding of yourself. He can grant you forgiveness and the gift of accepting yourself. He can take your talents and help develop and multiply them. He can bless you, and your children through you. All you have to do is *ask,* and then begin *working* for the changes.

Bless the Lord, O my soul;
>and all that is within me,
>bless his holy name!
Bless the Lord, O my soul,
>and forget not all his benefits,
who forgives all your iniquity,
>who heals all your diseases,

who redeems your life from the Pit,
>who crowns you with steadfast
>love and mercy,
who satisfies you with good
>as long as you live
>so that your youth is
>renewed like the eagle's. . . .

Bless the Lord, O my soul! (Ps. 103:1-5, 22)

A Final Word

I almost ran into a semi yesterday; I was watching some flashing lights in my rear view mirror. I couldn't tell if they represented a squad car, or fire engine, or ambulance, or what. But I watched them—an activity happening behind me, far behind me. It caught my attention. And I missed the semi by inches.

Halfway through this book I told a friend that I should title at least one chapter, "Dummy, You've Been Through This Before!" I have. Oh, I don't mean through two marriages. I mean through one life. I've done the same dumb things again and again. I've doubted; but more than that, I've forgotten. I've forgotten the past learning experiences, or just the opposite, I've been so caught up in the reruns—the rear view mirror—that I've almost collided again. When will I ever learn? I've been through this just yesterday, it seems, and still I react the same old way.

"For Demas . . . has deserted me and gone" (2 Tim. 4:10). Far earlier Paul had written the Colossians, "Luke the beloved physician and Demas greet you" (Col. 4:14). And in between: "Epaphras, my fellow prisoner in Christ Jesus, sends greetings to you; and so do Mark, Aristarchus, Demas, and Luke, my fellow

65714

workers" (Philemon 23). And finally, "Demas has deserted me. . . ."

There is nothing so glorious as a good beginning, and nothing so tragic as a bad ending!

Reading a book like this, any book, is a good beginning. Forgetting it, however it helped you at the moment, is human. We turn to God when we're in great pain; we tend to forget him when we're anesthetized.

"Sin boldly," said Luther. So you know what a sinner you are. So you stay in the state of needing God. So you can turn to him and pray:

Dear Lord,

Stay with me even when I leave you. I thank you for everything you've taught me through this experience. I'm going to make it, thanks to you. My children are going to make it, thanks to you. And you'll make our lives richer.

But when I forget you, and I surely will—or at least I'll stop feeling this intensity of you—please don't forget me. I'm just a child, and I'll never totally conceive, or understand, or appreciate, what you've done for me and for my youngsters. I can only thank you and pray that I never leave you, and more important, that you never leave me.

"May the God of hope fill you with all joy and peace in believing, so that by the power of the Holy Spirit, you may abound in hope" (Rom. 15:13).